Parochial and Plain Sermons
by John Henry Newman

Address:
HardPress
8345 NW 66TH ST #2561
MIAMI FL 33166-2626
USA
Email: info@hardpress.net

PAROCHIAL AND PLAIN SERMONS

VOLUME VII.

RIVINGTONS

London ...	...	...	...	...	...	*Waterloo Place*
Oxford ...	...	...	...	...	...	*High Street*
Cambridge	...	...	...	...	...	*Trinity Street*

PAROCHIAL AND PLAIN SERMONS

By JOHN HENRY NEWMAN, B.D.

FORMERLY VICAR OF ST. MARY'S, OXFORD

IN EIGHT VOLUMES

VOL. VII.

NEW EDITION

RIVINGTONS
London, Oxford, and Cambridge
1868

CONTENTS.

Contents.

SERMON XVIII.

STEDFASTNESS IN THE OLD PATHS.

𝔍𝔢𝔯𝔢𝔪𝔦𝔞𝔥 vi. 16.

SERMON I.

THE LAPSE OF TIME.

ECCLES. ix. 10.

" Whatsoever thy hand findeth to do, do it with thy might; for there is no work, nor device, nor knowledge, nor wisdom, in the grave, whither thou goest." Salvation of souls the TRUE WORK

SOLOMON'S advice that we should do whatever our hand findeth to do with our might, naturally directs our thoughts to that great work in which all others are included, which will outlive all other works, and for which alone we really are placed here below—the salvation of our souls. And the consideration of this great work, which must be done with all our might, and completed before the grave, whither we go, presents itself to our minds with especial force at the commencement of a new year. We are now entering on a fresh stage of our life's journey; we know well how it will end, and we see where we shall stop in the evening, though we do not see the road. And we know in what our business lies while we travel, and that it is important for us to do it with our " might; for there is no. work, nor device, nor

[VII]   B knowledge, nor wisdom, in the grave." This is so plain, that nothing need be said in order to convince us that it is true. We know it well; the very complaint which numbers commonly make when told of it, is that they know it already, that it is nothing new, that they have no need to be told, and that it is tiresome to hear the same thing said over and over again, and impertinent in the person who repeats it. Yes; thus it is that sinners silence their conscience, by quarrelling with those who appeal to it; they defend themselves, if it may be called a defence, by pleading that they already know what they should do and do not; that they know perfectly well that they are living at a distance from God, and are in peril of eternal ruin; that they know they are making themselves children of Satan, and denying the Lord that bought them, and want no one to tell them so. Thus they witness against themselves.

However, though we already know well enough that we have much to do before we die, yet (if we will but attend) it may be of use to hear the fact dwelt upon; because by thinking over it steadily and seriously, we may possibly, through God's grace, gain some deep conviction of it; whereas while we keep to general terms, and confess that this life is important and is short, in the mere summary way in which men commonly confess it, we have, properly speaking, no knowledge of that great truth at all.

Consider, then, what it is to die; " there is no work, device, knowledge, or wisdom, in the grave." Death puts an end absolutely and irrevocably to all our plans and works, and it is inevitable. The Psalmist speaks to " high and low, rich and poor, one with another." " No man can deliver his brother, nor make agreement unto God for him." Even " wise men die, as well as the ignorant and foolish, and leave their riches for other[1]." Difficult as we may find it to bring it home to ourselves, to realize it, yet as surely as we are here assembled together, so surely will every one of us, sooner or later, one by one, be stretched on the bed of death. We naturally shrink from the thought of death, and of its attendant circumstances; but all that is hateful and fearful about it will be fulfilled in our case, one by one. But all this is nothing compared with the consequences implied in it. Death stops us; it stops our race. Men are engaged about their work, or about their pleasure; they are in the city, or the field; any how they are stopped; their deeds are suddenly gathered in—a reckoning is made— all is sealed up till the great day. What a change is this! In the words used familiarly in speaking of the dead, they are no more. They were full of schemes and projects; whether in a greater or humbler rank, they had their hopes and fears, their prospects, their pursuits, their rivalries; all these are now come to an end. One builds a house, and its roof is not finished; another

[1] Ps. xlix. 2—10.

buys merchandise, and it is not yet sold. And all their virtues and pleasing qualities which endeared them to their friends are, as far as this world is concerned, vanished. Where are they who were so active, so sanguine, so generous? the amiable, the modest, and the kind? We were told that they were dead; they suddenly disappeared; that is all we know about it. They were silently taken from us; they are not met in the seat of the elders, nor in the assemblies of the people; in the mixed concourse of men, nor in the domestic retirement which they prized. As Scripture describes it, " the wind has passed over them, and they are gone, and their place shall know them no more." And they have burst the many ties which held them; they were parents, brothers, sisters, children, and friends; but the bond of kindred is broken, and the silver cord of love is loosed. They have been followed by the vehement grief of tears, and the long sorrow of aching hearts; but they make no return, they answer not; they do not even satisfy our wish to know that they sorrow for us as we for them. We talk about them thenceforth as if they were persons we do not know; we talk about them as third persons; whereas they used to be always with us, and every other thought which was within us was shared by them. Or perhaps, if our grief is too deep, we do not mention their names at all. And their possessions, too, all fall to others. The world goes on without them; it forgets them. Yes, so it is;

The Lapse of Time. 5

the world contrives to forget that men have souls, it looks upon them all as mere parts of some great visible system. This continues to move on; to this the world ascribes a sort of life and personality. When one or other of its members die, it considers them only as falling out of the system, and as come to nought. For a minute, perhaps, it thinks of them in sorrow, then leaves them—leaves them for ever. It keeps its eye on things seen and temporal. Truly whenever a man dies, rich or poor, an immortal soul passes to judgment; but somehow we read of the deaths of persons we have seen or heard of, and this reflection never comes across us. Thus does the world really cast off men's souls, and recognizing only their bodies, it makes it appear as if "that which befalleth the sons of men befalleth beasts, even one thing befalleth them, as the one dieth so dieth the other; yea, they have all one breath, so that a man hath no pre-eminence over a beast, for all is vanity[1]."

But let us follow the course of a soul thus casting off the world, and cast off by it. It goes forth as a stranger on a journey. Man seems to die and to be no more, when he is but quitting us, and is really beginning to live. Then he sees sights which before it did not even enter into his mind to conceive, and the world is even less to him than he to the world. Just now he was lying on the bed of sickness, but in that moment of

[1] Eccles. iii. 19.

death what an awful change has come over him! What a crisis for him! There is stillness in the room that lately held him; nothing is doing there, for he is gone, he now belongs to others; he now belongs entirely to the Lord who bought him; to Him he returns; but whether to be lodged safely in His place of hope, or to be imprisoned against the great Day, that is another matter, that depends on the deeds done in the body, whether good or evil. And now what are his thoughts? How infinitely important now appears the value of time, now when it is nothing to him! Nothing; for though he spend centuries waiting for Christ, he cannot now alter his state from bad to good, or from good to bad. What he dieth that he must be for ever; as the tree falleth so must it lie. This is the comfort of the true servant of God, and the misery of the transgressor. His lot is cast once and for all, and he can but wait in hope or in dread. Men on their death-beds have declared, that no one could form a right idea of the value of time till he came to die; but if this has truth in it, how much more truly can it be said after death! What an estimate shall we form of time while we are waiting for judgment! Yes, it is we — all this, I repeat, belongs to us most intimately. It is not to be looked at as a picture, as a man might read a light book in a leisure hour. *We* must die, the youngest, the healthiest, the most thoughtless; *we* must be thus unnaturally torn in two, soul from body; and only united again to be

POWERFUL THOUGHT

made more thoroughly happy or to be miserable for ever.

Such is death considered in its inevitable necessity, and its unspeakable importance—nor can we ensure to ourselves any certain interval before its coming. The time may be long; but it may also be short. It is plain, a man may die any day; all we can say is, that it is unlikely that he will die. But of this, at least, we are certain, that, come it sooner or later, death is continually on the move towards us. We are ever nearer and nearer to it. Every morning we rise we are nearer that grave in which there is no work, nor device, than we were. We are now nearer the grave, than when we entered this Church. Thus life is ever crumbling away under us. What should we say to a man, who was placed on some precipitous ground, which was ever crumbling under his feet, and affording less and less secure footing, yet was careless about it? Or what should we say to one who suffered some precious liquor to run from its receptacle into the thoroughfare of men, without a thought to stop it? who carelessly looked on and saw the waste of it, becoming greater and greater every minute? But what treasure can equal time? It is the seed of eternity : yet we suffer ourselves to go on, year after year, hardly using it at all in God's service, or thinking it enough to give Him at most a tithe or a seventh of it, while we strenuously and heartily sow to the flesh, that from the flesh we may reap corruption.

TIME is the SEED of ETERNITY

We try how little we can safely give to religion, instead of having the grace to give abundantly. " Rivers of water run down mine eyes, because men keep not Thy law ;" so says the holy Psalmist. Doubtless an inspired prophet saw far more clearly than we can see, the madness of men in squandering that treasure upon sin, which is meant to buy their chief good ;—but if so, what must this madness appear in God's sight ! What an inveterate malignant evil is it in the hearts of the sons of men, that thus leads them to sit down to eat, and drink, and rise up to play, when time is hurrying on and judgment coming ? We have been told what He thinks of man's unbelief, though we cannot enter into the depths of His thoughts. He showed it to us in act and deed, as far as we could receive it, when He even sent His Only-begotten Son into the world as at this time, to redeem us from the world,—which, most surely, was not lightly done ; and we also learn His thoughts about it from the words of that most merciful Son,—which most surely were not lightly spoken, " The wicked," He says, " shall go into everlasting punishment."

Oh that there were such a heart in us that we would fear God and keep His commandments always ! But it is of no use to speak ; men know their duty—they will not do it. They say they do not need or wish to be told it, that it is an intrusion, and a rudeness, to tell them of death and judgment. So must it be,—and we, who have to speak to them, must submit to this. Speak we must, as an act of duty to God, whether they will hear, or not, and then must leave our words as a witness. Other means for rousing them we have none. We speak from Christ our gracious Lord, their Redeemer, who has already pardoned them freely, yet they will not follow Him with a true heart; and what can be done more?

Another year is now opening upon us; it speaks to the thoughtful, and is heard by those, who have expectant ears, and watch for Christ's coming. The former year is gone, it is dead, there it lies in the grave of past time, not to decay however, and be forgotten, but kept in the view of God's omniscience, with all its sins and errors irrevocably written, till, at length, it will be raised again to testify about us at the last day; and who among us can bear the thought of his own doings, in the course of it?—all that he has said and done, all that has been conceived within his mind, or been acted on, and all that he has not said and done, which it was a duty to say or do. What a dreary prospect seems to be before us, when we reflect that we have the solemn word of truth pledged to us, in the last and most awful revelation, which God has made to us about the future, that in that day, the books will be opened, "and another book opened, which is the book of life, and the dead judged out of those things which were written in the books according to their works[1]!" What would a man

[1] Rev. xx. 12.

give, any one of us, who has any real insight into his
polluted and miserable state, what would he give to tear
away some of the leaves there preserved! For how
heinous are the sins therein written! Think of the
multitude of sins done by us since we first knew the
difference between right and wrong. We have forgotten
them, but there we might read them clearly recorded.
Well may holy David exclaim, " Remember not the sins
of my youth nor my transgressions, according to Thy
mercy remember Thou me." Conceive, too, the multitude of sins which have so grown into us as to become
part of us, and in which we now live, not knowing, or
but partially knowing, that they are sins; habits of
pride, self-reliance, self-conceit, sullenness, impurity, sloth,
selfishness, worldliness. The history of all these, their
beginnings, and their growth, is recorded in those dreadful books; and when we look forward to the future, how
many sins shall we have committed by this time next
year,—though we try ever so much to know our duty,
and overcome ourselves! Nay, or rather shall we have
the opportunity of obeying or disobeying God for a year
longer? Who knows whether by that time our account
may not be closed for ever?

" Remember me, O Lord, when Thou comest into
Thy kingdom [1]." Such was the prayer of the penitent
thief on the cross, such must be our prayer. Who can
do us any good, but He, who shall also be our Judge?

[1] Luke xxiii. 42.

PRAYER of the THIEF
PRAYER of the PUBLICAN

When shocking thoughts about ourselves come across us and afflict us, " Remember me," this is all we have to say. We have " no work, nor device, nor knowledge, nor wisdom " of our own, to better ourselves withal. We can say nothing to God in defence of ourselves,— we can but acknowledge that we are grievous sinners, and addressing Him as suppliants, merely beg Him to bear us in mind in mercy, for His Son's sake to do us some favour, not according to our deserts, but for the love of Christ. The more we try to serve Him here, the better; but after all, so far do we fall short of what we should be, that if we had but what we are in our-selves to rely upon, wretched are we,—and we are forced out of ourselves by the very necessity of our condition. To whom should we go? Who can do us any good, but He who was born into this world for our regenera-tion, was bruised for our iniquities, and rose again for our justification? Even though we have served Him from our youth up, though after His pattern we have grown, as far as mere man can grow, in wisdom as we grew in stature, though we ever have had tender hearts, and a mortified will, and a conscientious temper, and an obe-dient spirit; yet, at the very best, how much have we left undone, how much done, which ought to be other-wise! What He can do for our nature, in the way of sanctifying it, we know indeed in a measure; we know, in the case of His saints; and we certainly do not know the limit of His carrying forward in those objects of

His special favour the work of purification, and renewal through His Spirit. But for ourselves, we know full well that much as we may have attempted, we have done very little, that our very best service is nothing worth,—and the more we attempt, the more clearly we shall see how little we have hitherto attempted.

Those whom Christ saves are they who at once attempt to save themselves, yet despair of saving themselves; who aim to do all, and confess they do nought; who are all love, and all fear; who are the most holy, and yet confess themselves the most sinful; who ever seek to please Him, yet feel they never can; who are full of good works, yet of works of penance. All this seems a contradiction to the natural man, but it is not so to those whom Christ enlightens. They understand in proportion to their illumination, that it is possible to work out their salvation, yet to have it wrought out for them, to fear and tremble at the thought of judgment, yet to rejoice always in the Lord, and hope and pray for His coming.

The Paradox of the
Christian Life

SERMON II.

RELIGION A WEARINESS TO THE NATURAL MAN.

ISAIAH liii. 2.

" He hath no form nor comeliness; and when we shall see Him, there is no beauty that we should desire Him."

"RELIGION is a weariness;" such is the judgment commonly passed, often avowed, concerning the greatest of blessings which Almighty God has bestowed upon us. And when God gave the blessing, He at the same time foretold that such would be the judgment of the world upon it, even as manifested in the gracious Person of Him whom He sent to give it to us. "He hath no form nor comeliness," says the Prophet, speaking of our Lord and Saviour, "and when we shall see Him, there is no beauty that we should desire Him." He declared beforehand, that to man His religion would be uninteresting and distasteful. Not that this prediction excuses our deadness to it; this dislike of the religion given us by God Himself, seen as it is on all sides of us,—of religion in all its parts, whether its doctrines, its

precepts, its polity, its worship, its social influence,
—this distaste for its very name, must obviously be
an insult to the Giver. But the text speaks of it
as a fact, without commenting on the guilt involved
in it; and as such I wish you to consider it, as far
as this may be done in reverence and seriousness.
Putting aside for an instant the thought of the in-
gratitude and the sin which indifference to Christianity
implies, let us, as far as we dare, view it merely as
a matter of fact, after the manner of the text, and
form a judgment on the probable consequences of it.
Let us take the state of the case as it is found, and
survey it dispassionately, as even an unbeliever might
survey it, without at the moment considering whether
it is sinful or not; as a misfortune, if we will, or a
strange accident, or a necessary condition of our nature,
—one of the phenomena, as it may be called, of the
present world.

Let me then review human life in some of its stages
and conditions, in order to impress upon you the fact
of this contrariety between ourselves and our Maker:
He having one will, we another; He declaring one
thing to be good for us, and we fancying other objects
to be our good.

1. "Religion is a weariness;" alas! so feel even
children before they can well express their meaning.
Exceptions of course now and then occur; and of course
children are always more open to religious impressions

and visitations than grown persons. They have many good thoughts and good desires, of which, in after life, the multitude of men seem incapable. Yet who, after all, can have a doubt that, in spite of the more intimate presence of God's grace with those who have not yet learned to resist it, still, on the whole, religion is a weariness to children? Consider their amusements, their enjoyments,—what they hope, what they devise, what they scheme, and what they dream about themselves in time future, when they grow up; and say what place religion holds in their hearts. Watch the reluctance with which they turn to religious duties, to saying their prayers, or reading the Bible; and then judge. Observe, as they get older, the influence which the fear of the ridicule of their companions has in deterring them even from speaking of religion, or seeming to be religious. Now the dread of ridicule, indeed, is natural enough; but why should religion inspire ridicule? What is there absurd in thinking of God? Why should we be ashamed of worshipping Him? It is unaccountable, but it is natural. We may call it an accident, or what we will; still it is an undeniable fact, and that is what I insist upon. I am not forgetful of the peculiar character of children's minds : sensible objects first meet their observation; it is not wonderful that they should at first be inclined to limit their thoughts to things of sense. A distinct profession of faith, and a conscious maintenance of principle, may imply a strength and consistency of thought to which they are as yet unequal. Again, childhood is capricious, ardent, light-hearted; it cannot think deeply or long on any subject. Yet all this is not enough to account for the fact in question—why they should feel this distaste for the very subject of religion. Why should they be ashamed of paying reverence to an unseen, all-powerful God, whose existence they do not disbelieve? Yet they do feel ashamed of it. Is it that they are ashamed of themselves, not of their religion; feeling the inconsistency of professing what they cannot fully practise? This refinement does not materially alter the view of the case; for it is merely their own acknowledgment that they do not love religion as much as they ought. No; we seem compelled to the conclusion, that there is by nature some strange discordance between what we love and what God loves. So much, then, on the state of boyhood.

2. "Religion is a weariness." I will next take the case of young persons when they first enter into life. Here I may appeal to some perhaps who now hear me. Alas! my brethren, is it not so? Is not religion associated in your minds with gloom, melancholy, and weariness? I am not at present going so far as to reprove you for it, though I might well do so; if I did, perhaps you might at once turn away, and I wish you calmly to think the matter over,

and bear me witness that I state the fact correctly. It is so; you cannot deny it. The very terms "religion," "devotion," "piety," "conscientiousness," "mortification," and the like, you find to be inexpressibly dull and cheerless: you cannot find fault with them, indeed, you would if you could; and whenever the words are explained in particulars and realized, then you do find occasion for exception and objection. But though you cannot deny the claims of religion used as a vague and general term, yet how irksome, cold, uninteresting, uninviting, does it at best appear to you! how severe its voice! how forbidding its aspect! With what animation, on the contrary, do you enter into the mere pursuits of time and the world! What bright anticipations of joy and happiness flit before your eyes! How you are struck and dazzled at the view of the prizes of this life, as they are called! How you admire the elegancies of art, the brilliance of wealth, or the force of intellect! According to your opportunities you mix in the world, you meet and converse with persons of various conditions and pursuits, and are engaged in the numberless occurrences of daily life. You are full of news; you know what this or that person is doing, and what has befallen him; what has not happened, which was near happening, what may happen. You are full of ideas and feelings upon all that goes on around you. But, from some cause or other, religion has no part, no sensible influence, in your judgment of men and things. It is out of your way. Perhaps you have your pleasure parties; you readily take your share in them time after time; you pass continuous hours in society where you know that it is quite impossible even to mention the name of religion. Your heart is in scenes and places when conversation on serious subjects is strictly forbidden by the rules of the world's propriety. I do not say we should discourse on religious subjects, wherever we go; I do not say we should make an effort to discourse on them at any time, nor that we are to refrain from social meetings in which religion does not lie on the surface of the conversation: but I do say, that when men find their pleasure and satisfaction to lie in society which proscribes religion, and when they deliberately and habitually prefer those amusements which have necessarily nothing to do with religion, such persons cannot view religion as God views it. And this is the point: that the feelings of our hearts on the subject of religion are different from the declared judgment of God; that we have a natural distaste for that which He has said is our chief good.

3. Now let us pass to the more active occupations of life. Here, too, religion is confessedly felt to be wearisome, it is out of place. The transactions of worldly business, speculations in trade, ambitious hopes, the pursuit of knowledge, the public occurrences of the day, these find a way directly to the heart; they rouse, they

influence. It is superfluous to go about to prove this innate power over us of things of time and sense, to make us think and act. The name of religion, on the other hand, is weak and impotent; it contains no spell to kindle the feelings of man, to make the heart beat with anxiety, and to produce activity and perseverance. The reason is not merely that men are in want of leisure, and are sustained in a distressing continuance of exertion, by their duties towards those dependent on them. They have their seasons of relaxation, they turn for a time from their ordinary pursuits; still religion does not attract them, they find nothing of comfort or satisfaction in it. For a time they allow themselves to be idle. They want an object to employ their minds upon; they pace to and fro in very want of an object; yet their duties to God, their future hopes in another state of being, the revelation of God's mercy and will, as contained in Scripture, the news of redemption, the gift of regeneration, the sanctities, the devotional heights, the nobleness and perfection which Christ works in His elect, do not suggest themselves as fit subjects to dispel their weariness. Why? Because religion makes them melancholy, say they, and they wish to relax. Religion is a labour, it is a weariness, a greater weariness than the doing nothing at all. "Wherefore," says Solomon, "is there a price in the hand of a fool to get wisdom, seeing he hath no heart to it[1]?"

[1] Prov. xvii. 16.

4. But this natural contrariety between man and his Maker is still more strikingly shown by the confessions of men of the world who have given some thought to the subject, and have viewed society with somewhat of a philosophical spirit. Such men treat the demands of religion with disrespect and negligence, on the ground of their being unnatural. They say, " It is natural for men to love the world for its own sake; to be engrossed in its pursuits, and to set their hearts on the rewards of industry, on the comforts, luxuries, and pleasures of this life. Man would not be man if he could be made otherwise ; he would not be what he was evidently intended for by his Maker." Let us pass by the obvious *answer* that might be given to this objection ; it is enough for my purpose that it is *commonly urged*, recognizing as it does the fact of the disagreement existing between the claims of God's word, and the inclinations and natural capacities of man. Many, indeed, of those unhappy men who have denied the Christian faith, treat the religious principle altogether as a mere unnatural, eccentric state of mind, a peculiar untoward condition of the affections to which weakness will reduce a man, whether it has been brought on by anxiety, oppressive sorrow, bodily disease, excess of imagination or the like, and temporary or permanent, according to the circumstances of the disposing cause ; a state to which we all are liable, as we are liable to any other mental injury, but unmanly and unworthy of our dignity as rational beings. Here again it is enough for

our purpose, that it is allowed by these persons that the love of religion is unnatural and inconsistent with the original condition of our minds.

The same remark may be made upon the notions which secretly prevail in certain quarters at the present day, concerning the unsuitableness of Christianity to an enlightened age. Men there are who look upon the inspired word of God with a sort of indulgence, as if it had its use, and had done service in its day; that in times of ignorance it awed and controlled fierce barbarians, whom nothing else could have subdued; but that from its very claim to be divine and infallible, and its consequent unalterableness, it is an obstacle to the improvement of the human race beyond a certain point, and must ultimately fall before the gradual advancement of mankind in knowledge and virtue. In other words, the literature of the day is weary of Revealed Religion.

5. Once more; that religion is in itself a weariness is seen even in the conduct of the better sort of persons, who really on the whole are under the influence of its spirit. So dull and uninviting is calm and practical religion, that religious persons are ever exposed to the temptation of looking out for excitements of one sort or other, to make it pleasurable to them. The spirit of the Gospel is a meek, humble, gentle, unobtrusive spirit. It doth not cry nor lift up its voice in the streets, unless called upon by duty so to do, and then it does it with pain. Display, pretension, conflict, are unpleasant to it.

What then is to be thought of persons who are ever on the search after novelties to make religion interesting to them; who seem to find that Christian activity cannot be kept up without unchristian party-spirit, or Christian conversation without unchristian censoriousness? Why, this; that religion is to them as to others, taken by itself, a weariness, and requires something foreign to its own nature to make it palatable. Truly it is a weariness to the natural man to serve God humbly and in obscurity; it is very wearisome, and very monotonous, to go on day after day watching all we do and think, detecting our secret failings, denying ourselves, creating within us, under God's grace, those parts of the Christian character in which we are deficient; wearisome to learn modesty, love of insignificance, willingness to be thought little of, backwardness to clear ourselves when slandered, and readiness to confess when we are wrong; to learn to have no cares for this world, neither to hope nor to fear, but to be resigned and contented!

I may close these remarks, by appealing to the consciences of all who have ever set about the work of religion in good earnest, whoever they may be, whether they have made less, or greater progress in their noble toil, whether they are matured saints, or feeble strugglers against the world and the flesh. They have ever confessed how great efforts were necessary to keep close to the commandments of God; in spite of their knowledge of the truth, and their faith, in spite of the aids and consolations they receive from above, still how often do their corrupt hearts betray them !   Even their privileges are often burdensome to them, even to pray for the grace which in Christ is pledged to them is an irksome task.   They know that God's service is perfect freedom, and they are convinced, both in their reason and from their own experience of it, that it is true happiness; still they confess withal the strange reluctance of their nature to love their Maker and His Service.   And this is the point in question; not only the mass of mankind, but even the confirmed servants of Christ, witness to the opposition which exists between their own nature and the demands of religion.

This then is the remarkable fact which I proposed to show.   Can we doubt that man's will runs contrary to God's will — that the view which the inspired word takes of our present life, and of our destiny, does not satisfy us, as it rightly ought to do? that Christ hath no form nor comeliness in our eyes; and though we see Him, we see no desirable beauty in Him?   That holy, merciful, and meek Saviour, the Eternal, the Only-begotten Son of God, our friend and infinite benefactor—He who left the glory of His Father and died for us, who has promised us the overflowing riches of His grace both here and hereafter, He is a light shining in a dark place, and "the darkness comprehendeth it not." "Light is come into the world, and men love darkness rather than light."   The nature of man is flesh, and that which is born of the flesh is flesh, and ever must so remain; it never can discern, love, accept, the holy doctrines of the Gospel. It will occupy itself in various ways, it will take interest in things of sense and time, but it can never be religious. It is at enmity with God.

And now we see what must at once follow from what has been said. If our hearts are by nature set on the world for its own sake, and the world is one day to pass away, what are they to be set on, what to delight in, then? Say, how will the soul feel when, stripped of its present attire, which the world bestows, it stands naked and shuddering before the pure, tranquil, and severe majesty of the Lord its God, its most merciful, yet dishonoured Maker and Saviour? What are to be the pleasures of the soul in another life? Can they be the same as they are here? They cannot; Scripture tells us they cannot; the world passeth away—now what is there left to love and enjoy through a long eternity? What a dark, forlorn, miserable eternity that will be!

It is then plain enough, though Scripture said not a word on the subject, that if we would be happy in the world to come, we must make us new hearts, and begin to love the things we naturally do not love. Viewing it as a practical point, the end of the whole matter is this, we must be changed; for we cannot, we cannot expect the system of the universe to come over to us;

the inhabitants of heaven, the numberless creations of Angels, the glorious company of the Apostles, the goodly fellowship of the Prophets, the noble army of Martyrs, the holy Church universal, the Will and Attributes of God, these are fixed. We must go over to them. In our Saviour's own authoritative words: " Verily, verily, except a man be born again, he cannot see the kingdom of God[1]." It is a plain matter of self-interest, to turn our thoughts to the means of changing our hearts, putting out of the question our duty towards God and Christ, our Saviour and Redeemer.

" He hath no form nor comeliness, and when we see Him, there is no beauty that we should desire Him." It is not His loss that we love Him not, it is our loss. He is All-blessed, whatever becomes of us. He is not less blessed because we are far from Him. It is we who are not blessed, except as we approach Him, except as we are like Him, except as we love Him. Woe unto us, if in the day in which He comes from Heaven we see nothing desirable or gracious in His wounds; but instead, have made for ourselves an ideal blessedness, different from that which will be manifested to us in Him. Woe unto us, if we have made pride, or selfishness, or the carnal mind, our standard of perfection and truth; if our eyes have grown dim, and our hearts gross, as regards the true light of men, and the glory of the Eternal Father. May He Himself

[1] John iii. 8.

save us from our self-delusions, whatever they are, and enable us to give up this world, that we may gain the next;—and to rejoice in Him, who had no home of His own, no place to lay His head, who was poor and lowly, and despised and rejected, and tormented and slain !

SERMON III.

THE WORLD OUR ENEMY.

1 JOHN v. 19.

" We know that we are of God, and the whole world lieth in wickedness."

FEW words are of more frequent occurrence in the language of religion than " the world;" Holy Scripture makes continual mention of it, in the way of censure and caution ; in the Service for Baptism it is described as one of three great enemies of our souls; and in the ordinary writings and conversation of Christians, I need hardly say, mention is made of it continually.   Yet most of us, it would appear, have very indistinct notions what the world means.   We know that the world is a something dangerous to our spiritual interests, and that it is in some way connected with human society—with men as a mixed multitude, contrasted with men one by one, in private and domestic life ; but what it is, how it is our enemy, how it attacks, and how it is to be avoided, is not so clear.   Or if we conceive some distinct notion concerning it, still probably it is a wrong notion,—which

leads us, in consequence, to misapply the Scripture precepts relating to the world; and this is even worse than
overlooking them. I shall now, then, attempt to show
what is meant by the world, and how, in consequence,
we are to understand the information and warnings of
the sacred writers concerning it.

1. Now, first, by the world is very commonly meant
the present visible system of things, without taking into
consideration whether it is good or bad. Thus St. John
contrasts the world with the things that are in it, which
are evil, " Love not the world, *neither* the things that are
in the world [1]." Again, he presently says, " The world
passeth away, *and* the lust thereof." Here, as in many
other parts of Scripture, the world is not spoken of as
actually sinful in itself (though its lusts are so, of
course), but merely as some present visible system which
is likely to attract us, and is not to be trusted, because
it cannot last. Let us first consider it in this point of
view.

There is, as a matter of necessity, a great variety of
stations and fortunes among mankind; hardly two persons are in the same outward circumstances, and possessed of the same mental resources. Men differ from
each other, and are bound together into one body or
system by the very points in which they differ; they
depend on each other; such is the will of God. This
system is the world, to which it is plain belong

---

[1] 1 John ii. 15.

our various modes of supporting ourselves and families by exertion of mind and body, our intercourse with others, our duty towards others, the social virtues,—industry, honesty, prudence, justice, benevolence, and the like. These spring all from our present lot in life, and tend to our present happiness. This life holds out prizes to merit and exertion. Men rise above their fellows; they gain fame and honours, wealth and power, which we therefore call worldly goods. The affairs of nations, the dealings of people with people, the interchange of productions between country and country, are of this world. We are educated in boyhood for this world; we play our part on a stage more or less conspicuous, as the case may be; we die, we are no more, we are forgotten, as far as the present state of things is concerned; all this is of the world.

By the world, then, is meant this course of things which we see carried on by means of human agency, with all its duties and pursuits. It is not necessarily a sinful system; rather it is framed, as I have said, by God Himself, and therefore cannot be otherwise than good. And yet even thus considering it, we are bid not to love the world: even in this sense the world is an enemy of our souls; and for this reason, because the love of it is dangerous to beings circumstanced as we are,—things in themselves good being not good to us sinners. And this state of things which we see, fair and excellent in itself, is very likely (for the very reason that it is seen, and because the spiritual and future world is not seen) to seduce our wayward hearts from our true and eternal good.   As the traveller on serious business may be tempted to linger, while he gazes on the beauty of the prospect which opens on his way, so this well-ordered and divinely-governed world, with all its blessings of sense and knowledge, may lead us to neglect those interests which will endure when itself has passed away.   In truth, it promises more than it can fulfil.   The goods of life and the applause of men have their excellence, and, as far as they go, are really good; but they are short-lived.   And hence it is that many pursuits in themselves honest and right, are nevertheless to be engaged in with caution, lest they seduce us; and those perhaps with especial caution, which tend to the well-being of men in this life.   The sciences, for instance, of good government, of acquiring wealth, of preventing and relieving want, and the like, are for this reason especially dangerous; for fixing, as they do, our exertions on this world as an end, they go far to persuade us that they have no other end; they accustom us to think too much of success in life and temporal prosperity; nay, they may even teach us to be jealous of religion and its institutions, as if these stood in our way, preventing us from doing so much for the worldly interests of mankind as we might wish.

In this sense it is that St. Paul contrasts sight and faith.   We see this world; we only believe that there is a world of spirits, we do not see it: and inasmuch as sight has more power over us than belief, and the present than the future, so are the occupations and pleasures of this life injurious to our faith. Yet not, I say, in themselves sinful; as the Jewish system was a temporal system, yet divine, so is the system of nature— this world—divine, though temporal. And as the Jews became carnal-minded even by the influence of their divinely-appointed system, and thereby rejected the Saviour of their souls; in like manner, men of the world are hardened by God's own good world, into a rejection of Christ. In neither case through the fault of the things which are seen, whether miraculous or providential, but accidentally, through the fault of the human heart.

2. But now, secondly, let us proceed to consider the world, not only as dangerous, but as positively sinful, according to the text—" the whole world lieth in wickedness." It was created well in all respects, but even before it as yet had fully grown out into its parts, while as yet the elements of human society did but lie hid in the nature and condition of the first man, Adam fell; and thus the world, with all its social ranks, and aims, and pursuits, and pleasures, and prizes, has ever from its birth been sinful. The infection of sin spread through the whole system, so that although the frame-work is good and divine, the spirit and life within it are evil. Thus, for instance, to be in a high station is the gift of

God; but the pride and injustice to which it has given scope is from the Devil. To be poor and obscure is also the ordinance of God; but the dishonesty and discontent which are often seen in the poor is from Satan. To cherish and protect wife and family is God's appointment; but the love of gain, and the low ambition, which lead many a man to exert himself, are sinful. Accordingly, it is said in the text, "The world lieth in wickedness,"—it is plunged and steeped, as it were, in a flood of sin, not a part of it remaining as God originally created it, not a part pure from the corruptions with which Satan has disfigured it.

Look into the history of the world, and what do you read there? Revolutions and changes without number, kingdoms rising and falling; and when without crime? States are established by God's ordinance, they have their existence in the necessity of man's nature; but when was one ever established, nay, or maintained, without war and bloodshed? Of all natural instincts, what is more powerful than that which forbids us to shed our fellows' blood? We shrink with natural horror from the thought of a murderer; yet not a government has ever been settled, or a state acknowledged by its neighbours, without war and the loss of life; nay, more than this, not content with unjustifiable bloodshed, the guilt of which must lie somewhere, instead of lamenting it as a grievous and humiliating evil, the world has chosen to honour the conqueror with its amplest share of admiration. To become a hero, in the eyes of the world, it is almost necessary to break the laws of God and man. Thus the deeds of the world are matched by the opinions and principles of the world : it adopts bad doctrine to defend bad practice; it loves darkness because its deeds are evil.

And as the affairs of nations are thus depraved by our corrupt nature, so are all the appointments and gifts of Providence perverted in like manner. What can be more excellent than the vigorous and patient employment of the intellect; yet in the hands of Satan it gives birth to a proud philosophy. When St. Paul preached, the wise men of the world, in God's eyes, were but fools, for they had used their powers of mind in the cause of error; their reasonings even led them to be irreligious and immoral; and they despised the doctrine of a resurrection which they neither loved nor believed. And again, all the more refined arts of life have been disgraced by the vicious tastes of those who excelled in them ; often they have been consecrated to the service of idolatry ; often they have been made the instruments of sensuality and riot. But it would be endless to recount the manifold and complex corruption which man has introduced into the world which God made good; evil has preoccupied the whole of it, and holds fast its conquest. We know, indeed, that the gracious God revealed Himself to His sinful creatures very soon after Adam's fall. He showed His will to mankind again and again, and pleaded with them through many ages; till at length His Son was born into this sinful world in the form of man, and taught us how to please Him. Still, hitherto the good work has proceeded slowly: such is His pleasure. Evil had the start of good by many days; it filled the world, it holds it: it has the strength of possession, and it has its strength in the human heart; for though we cannot keep from approving what is right in our conscience, yet we love and encourage what is wrong; so that when evil was once set up in the world, it was secured in its seat by the unwillingness with which our hearts relinquish it.

And now I have described what is meant by the sinful world; that is, the world as corrupted by man, the course of human affairs viewed in its connexion with the principles, opinions, and practices which actually direct it. There is no mistaking these; they are evil; and of these it is that St. John says, "If any man love the world, the love of the Father is not in him. For all that is in the world, the lust of the flesh, and the lust of the eyes, and the pride of life, is not of the Father, but is of the world [1]."

The world then is the enemy of our souls; first, because, however innocent its pleasures, and praiseworthy its pursuits may be, they are likely to engross us, unless we are on our guard: and secondly, because in all its best pleasures, and noblest pursuits, the seeds of sin

[1] John ii. 15, 16.

have been sown; an enemy hath done this; so that it is
most difficult to enjoy the good without partaking of
the evil also. As an orderly system of various ranks,
with various pursuits and their several rewards, it is to
be considered not sinful indeed, but dangerous to us.
On the other hand, considered in reference to its
principles and actual practices, it is really a sinful
world. Accordingly, when we are bid in Scripture to
shun the world, it is meant that we must be cautious,
lest we love what is good in it too well, and lest we love
the bad at all.——However, there is a mistaken notion
sometimes entertained, that the world is some particular
set of persons, and that to shun the world is to shun
them; as if we could point out, as it were, with the
finger, what is the world, and thus could easily rid ourselves of one of our three great enemies. Men, who are
beset with this notion, are often great lovers of the world
notwithstanding, while they think themselves at a distance from it altogether. They love its pleasures, and
they yield to its principles, yet they speak strongly
against men of the world, and avoid them. They act
the part of superstitious people, who are afraid of seeing
evil spirits in what are considered haunted places, while
these spirits are busy at their hearts instead, and they
do not suspect it.

3. Here then is a question, which it will be well to
consider, viz. how far the world is a separate body from
the Church of God. The two are certainly contrasted

in the text, as elsewhere in Scripture. "We know that *we* are of God, and *the whole world* lieth in wickedness." Now the true account of this is, that the Church so far from being literally, and in fact, separate from the wicked world, is within it. The Church is a body, gathered together in the world, and in a process of separation from it. The world's power, alas! is over the Church, because the Church has gone forth into the world to save the world. All Christians are in the world, and of the world, so far as sin still has dominion over them; and not even the best of us is clean every whit from sin. Though then, in our idea of the two, and in their principles, and in their future prospects, the Church is one thing, and the world is another, yet in present matter of fact, the Church is of the world, not separate from it; for the grace of God has but partial possession even of religious men, and the best that can be said of us is, that we have two sides, a light side and a dark, and that the dark happens to be the outermost. Thus we form part of the world to each other, though we be not of the world. Even supposing there were a society of men influenced individually by Christian motives, still this society, viewed as a whole, would be a worldly one; I mean a society holding and maintaining many errors, and countenancing many bad practices. Evil ever floats at the top. And if we inquire why it is that the good in Christians is seen less than the bad? I answer, first, because there is less of it; and secondly, because evil forces itself upon general notice, and good does not. So that in a large body of men, each contributing his portion, evil displays itself on the whole conspicuously, and in all its diversified shapes. And thirdly, from the nature of things, the soul cannot be understood by any but God, and a religious spirit is in St. Peter's words, "the hidden man of the heart." It is only the actions of others which we see for the most part, and since there are numberless ways of doing wrong, and but one of doing right, and numberless ways too of regarding and judging the conduct of others, no wonder that even the better sort of men, much more the generality, are, and seem to be, so sinful. God only sees the circumstances under which a man acts, and why he acts in this way and not in that. God only sees perfectly the train of thought which preceded his action, the motive, and the reasons. And God alone (if aught is ill done, or sinfully) sees the deep contrition afterwards,—the habitual lowliness, then bursting forth into special self-reproach,—and the meek faith casting itself wholly upon God's mercy. Think for a moment, how many hours in the day every man is left wholly to himself and his God, or rather how few minutes he is in intercourse with others—consider this, and you will perceive how it is that the life of the Church is hid with God, and how it is that the outward conduct of the Church must necessarily look like the world, even far more than it really is like it, and how vain, in con-

sequence, the attempt is (which some make) of separating the world distinctly from the Church. Consider,
moreover, how much there is, while we are in the body,
to stand in the way of one mind communicating with
another.   We are imprisoned in the body, and our intercourse is by means of words, which feebly represent our
real feelings.   Hence the best motives and truest opinions
are misunderstood, and the most sound rules of conduct
misapplied by others.   And Christians are necessarily
more or less strange to each other; nay, and as far as
the appearance of things is concerned, almost mislead
each other, and are, as I have said, the world one to
another.   It is long, indeed, before we become at all
acquainted with each other, and we appear the one to
the other cold, or harsh, or capricious, or self-willed,
when we are not so.   So that it unhappily comes to
pass, that even good men retire from each other into
themselves, and to their God, as if retreating from the
rude world.

And if all this takes place in the case of the better
sort of men, how much more will it happen in the case
of those multitudes who are still unstable in faith and
obedience, half Christians, not having yet wrought
themselves into any consistent shape of opinion and
practice !   These, so far from showing the better part of
themselves, often affect to be worse even than they are.
Though they have secret fears and misgivings, and
God's grace pleads with their conscience, and seasons of

seriousness follow, yet they are ashamed to confess to each other their own seriousness, and they ridicule religious men lest they should be themselves ridiculed.

And thus, on the whole, the state of the case is as follows : that if we look through mankind in order to find out who make up the world, and who do not, we shall find none who are not of the world ; inasmuch as there are none who are not exposed to infirmity. So that if to shun the world is to shun some body of men so called, we must shun all men, nay, ourselves too— which is a conclusion which means nothing at all.

But let us, avoiding all refinements which lead to a display of words only, not to the improvement of our hearts and conduct, let us set to work practically ; and instead of attempting to judge of mankind on a large scale, and to settle deep questions, let us take what is close at hand and concerns ourselves, and make use of such knowledge as we can obtain. Are we tempted to neglect the worship of God for some temporal object ? this is of the world, and not to be admitted. Are we ridiculed for our conscientious conduct ? this again is a trial of the world, and to be withstood. Are we tempted to give too much time to our recreations ; to be idling when we should be working ; reading or talking when we should be busy in our temporal calling ; hoping for impossibilities, or fancying ourselves in some different state of life from our own ; over anxious of the good opinion of others ; bent upon getting the credit of industry, honesty, and prudence? all these are temptations of this world. Are we discontented with our lot, or are we over attached to it, and fretful and desponding when God recalls the good He has given? this is to be worldly-minded.

Look not about for the world as some vast and gigantic evil far off—its temptations are close to you, apt and ready, suddenly offered and subtle in their address. Try to bring down the words of Scripture to common life, and to recognize the evil in which this world lies, in your own hearts.

When our Saviour comes, He will destroy this world, even His own work, and much more the lusts of the world, which are of the evil one; then at length we must lose the world, even if we cannot bring ourselves to part with it now. And we shall perish with the world, if on that day its lusts are found within us. "The world passeth away, and the lust thereof, but he that doeth the will of God abideth for ever."

SERMON IV.

THE PRAISE OF MEN.

John xii. 43.

" They loved the praise of men more than the praise of God."

THIS is spoken of the chief rulers of the Jews, who,
though they believed in Christ's Divine mission,
were afraid to confess Him, lest they should incur temporal loss and shame from the Pharisees. The censure
passed by St. John on these persons is too often ap-
plicable to Christians at the present day; perhaps,
indeed, there is no one among us who has not at some
time or other fallen under it. We love the good
opinion of the world more than the approbation of Him
who created us, redeemed us, has regenerated us, and
who still preserves to us the opportunity of preparing
ourselves for His future presence. Such is too often
the case with us. It is well we should be aware that it
is so; it is well we should dwell upon it, and that we
should understand and feel that it is wrong, which many
men do not.

Now it is an obvious question, Why is it wrong to

love the praise of men? For it may be objected, that we are accustomed to educate the young by means of praise and blame; that we encourage them by kind words *from us,* that is, from man; and punish them for disobedience. If, then, it may be argued, it is right to regard the opinions of others concerning us in our youth, it cannot be in itself wrong to pay attention to it at any other period of life. This is true; but I do not say that the mere love of praise and fear of shame are evil: regard to the corrupt world's praise or blame, this is what is sinful and dangerous. St. John, in the text, implies that the praise of men was, at the time spoken of, in opposition to the praise of God. It *must* be wrong to prefer any thing to the will of God. To seek praise is in itself as little wrong, as it is wrong to hope, and to fear, and to love, and to trust; all depends upon the object hoped, or feared, or loved, or trusted; to seek the praise of good men is not wrong, any more than to love or to reverence good men; only wrong when it is in excess, when it interferes with the exercise of love and reverence towards God. Not wrong while we look on good men singly as instruments and servants of God; or, in the words of Scripture, while " we glorify God in them [1]." But to seek the praise of bad men, is in itself as wrong as to love the company of bad men, or to admire them. It is not, I say, merely the love of praise that is a sin, but love of the corrupt

[1] Gal. i. 24.

world's praise. This is the case with all our natural feelings and affections; they are all in themselves good, and implanted by God; they are sinful, because we have in us by nature a something more than them, viz. an evil principle which perverts them to a bad end. Adam, before his fall, felt, we may suppose, love, fear, hope, joy, dislike, as we do now; but then he felt them only when he ought, and as he ought; all was harmoniously attempered and rightly adjusted in his soul, which was at unity with itself. But, at the fall, this beautiful order and peace was broken up; the same passions remained, but their use and action were changed; they rushed into extremes, sometimes excessive, sometimes the reverse. Indignation was corrupted into wrath, self-love became selfishness, self-respect became pride, and emulation envy and jealousy. They were at variance with each other; pride struggled with self-interest, fear with desire. Thus his soul became a chaos, and needed a new creation. Moreover, as I have said, his affections were set upon unsuitable objects. The natural man looks to this world, the world is his god; faith, love, hope, joy, are not excited in his mind by things spiritual and divine, but by things seen and temporal.

Considering, then, that love of praise is not a bad principle in itself, it is plain that a parent may very properly teach his child to love his praise, and fear his blame, when that praise and blame are given in accordance with God's praise and blame, and made subservient to them. And, in like manner, if the world at large took a correct and religious view of things, then its praise and blame would in its place be valuable too. Did the world admire what God admires; did it account humility, for instance, a great virtue, and pride a great sin; did it condemn that spirit of self-importance and sensitiveness of disgrace, which calls itself a love of honour; did it think little of temporal prosperity, wealth, rank, grandeur, and power; did it condemn arrogant and irreverent disputing, the noisy, turbulent spirit of ambition, the love of war and conquest, and the perverse temper which leads to jealousy and hatred; did it prefer goodness and truth to gifts of the intellect; did it think little of quickness, wit, shrewdness, power of speech and general acquirements, and much of patience, meekness, gentleness, firmness, faith, conscientiousness, purity, forgiveness of injuries,—then there would be no sin in our seeking the world's praise; and though we still ought to love God's praise above all, yet we might love the praise of the world in its degree, for it would be nothing more nor less than the praise of good men. But since, alas! the contrary is the case, since the world (as Scripture tells us) "lieth in wickedness," and the principles and practices which prevail on all sides of us are not those which the All-holy God sanctions, we cannot lawfully seek the world's praise. We cannot serve two masters who are enemies the one to the other.

We are forbidden to love the world or any thing that is of the world, for it is not of the Father, but passeth away.

This is the reason why it is wrong to pursue the world's praise; viz. because we cannot have it and God's praise too. And yet, as the pursuit of it is wrong, so is it common,—for this reason : because God is unseen, and the world is seen ; because God's praise and blame are future, the world's are present ; because God's praise and blame are inward, and come quietly and without keenness, whereas the world's are very plain and intelligible, and make themselves felt.

Take, for instance, the case of the young, on (what is called) entering into life. Very many, indeed, there are, whether in a higher or lower station, who enter into the mixed society of others early; so early, that it might be thought they had hardly had time to acquire any previous knowledge of right and wrong, any standard of right and wrong, other than the world gives, any principles by which to fight against the world. And yet it cannot quite be so. Whatever is the first time persons hear evil, it is quite certain that good has been beforehand with them, and they have a something within them which tells them it is evil. And much more, if they have been blessed, as most men are, with the protection of parents, or the kind offices of teachers or of God's ministers, they generally have principles of duty more or less strongly imprinted on their minds;

and on their first intercourse with strangers they are shocked or frighted at seeing the improprieties and sins, which are openly countenanced. Alas! there are persons, doubtless (though God forbid it should be the case with any here present!), whose consciences have been so early trained into forgetfulness of religious duties, that they can hardly, or cannot at all, recollect the time I speak of; the time when they acted with the secret feeling that God saw them, saw all they did and thought. I will not fancy this to be the case with any who hear me. Rather, there are many of you, in different ranks and circumstances, who have, and ever have had, general impressions on your minds of the claims which religion has on you, but, at the same time, have been afraid of acting upon them, afraid of the opinion of the world, of what others would say if you set about obeying your conscience. Ridicule is a most powerful instrument in the hands of Satan, and it is most vividly felt by the young. If any one wishes to do his duty, it is most easy for the cold, the heartless, and the thoughtless, to find out harsh, or provoking, or ridiculous names to fix upon him. My brethren, so many of you as are sensitive of the laughter or contempt of the world, this is your cross; you must wear it, you must endure it patiently; it is the mark of your conformity to Christ; He despised the shame: you must learn to endure it, from the example and by the aid of your Saviour. You must love the praise of God more than the praise of men. It is the very trial suited to you, appointed for you, to establish you in the faith. You are not tempted with gain or ambition, but with ridicule. And be sure, that unless you withstand it, you cannot endure hardships as good soldiers of Jesus Christ, you will not endure other temptations which are to follow. How can you advance a step in your after and more extended course till the first difficulty is overcome? You need faith, and " a double-minded man," says St. James, " is unstable in all his ways." Moreover, be not too sure that all who show an inclination to ridicule you, feel exactly as they say. They speak with the loudest speaker; speak you boldly, and they will speak with you. They have very little of definite opinion themselves, or probably they even feel with you, though they speak against you. Very likely they have uneasy, unsatisfied consciences, though they seem to sin so boldly; and are as afraid of the world as you can be, nay, more so; they join in ridiculing you, lest others should ridicule them; or they do so in a sort of self-defence against the reproaches of their own consciences. Numbers in this bad world talk loudly against religion in order to encourage each other in sin, because they need encouragement. They are cowards, and rely on each other for support against their fears. They know they ought to be other than they are, but are glad to avail themselves of any thing that looks like argument, to overcome their consciences withal. And ridicule is a

kind of argument—such as it is; and numbers ridiculing together are a still stronger one—of the same
kind.   Any how, there are few indeed who will not feel
afterwards, in times of depression or alarm, that you are
right, and they themselves are wrong.   Those who
serve God faithfully have a friend of their own, in
each man's bosom, witnessing for them; even in those
who treat them ill.   And I suppose no young person
has been able, through God's mercy, to withstand the
world's displeasure, but has felt at this time or that,
that this is so, and in a little time will, with all humility,
have the comfort of feeling it while he is withstanding
the world.

But now supposing he has not had strength of mind to
withstand the world; but has gone the way of the world.
Suppose he has joined the multitude in saying and doing
what he should not.   We know the careless, thoughtless,
profane habits which most men live in, making light
of serious subjects, and being ashamed of godliness and
virtue; ashamed of going to church regularly, ashamed of
faith, ashamed of chastity, ashamed of innocence, ashamed
of obedience to persons in authority.   Supposing a person
has been one of these, and then through God's grace
repents.   It often pleases God, in the course of His
Providence, to rouse men to reflection by the occurrences
of life.   In such circumstances they certainly will have
a severe trial to stand against the world.   Nothing
is more painful in the case of such persons, than the

necessity often imposed upon them of acting contrary to the opinion and wishes of those with whom they have till now been intimate,—whom they have admired and followed. Intimacies have already been formed, and ties drawn tight, which it is difficult to sever. What is the person in question to do? rudely to break them at once? no. But is he to share in sins in which he formerly took part? no; whatever censure, contempt, or ridicule attaches to him in consequence. But what, then, is he to do? His task, I say, is painful and difficult, but he must not complain, for it is his own making; it is the natural consequence of his past neglect of God. So much is plain,—he must abstain from all sinful actions; not converse lightly or irreverently where formerly he was not unwilling so to do; not spend his time, as heretofore, in idleness or riot; avoid places whither he is not called by actual duty, which offer temptation to sin; observe diligently attendance on church; not idle away the Lord's Day in vanity, or worse; not add to the number of his acquaintance any thoughtless persons. All this is quite plain, and in doing this I know he will incur the ridicule of his companions. He will have much to bear. He must bear to be called names, to be thought a hypocrite, to be thought to be affecting something out of the way, to be thought desirous of recommending himself to this or that person. He must be prepared for malicious and untrue reports about himself; many other trials must he look for. They are his

portion. He must pray God to enable him to bear them
meekly. He must pray for himself, he must pray for
those who ridicule him. He has deserved ridicule. He
has nothing to boast of, if he bears it well. He has
nothing to boast of that he incurs it. He has nothing
to boast of, as if he were so much better than those who
ridicule him ; he was once as they are now. He is now
just a little better than they are. He has just begun a
new life. He has got a very little way in it, or rather
no way, nothing beyond professing it ; and he has the
reproach of the world in consequence of his profession.
Well, let him see to it that this reproach is not in vain,
that he has a right to the reproach. Let him see to it
that he acts as well as professes. It will be miserable
indeed if he incurs the reproach, and yet does not gain
the reward. Let him pray God to perfect in him what
He has begun in him, and to begin and perfect it also
in all those that reproach him. Let him pray for
Christ's grace to bear hardships in Christ's spirit ; to be
able to look calmly in the world's face, and bear its
frown ; to trust in the Lord, and be doing good ; to
obey God, and so to be reproached, not for professing
only, but for performing, not for doing nothing, but for
doing something, and in God's cause. If we *are* under
reproach, let us have something to show for it. At
present, such a one is but a child in the Gospel ; but in
time, St. Peter's words will belong to him, and he may
appropriate them. " This is thankworthy, if a man for

conscience towards God endure grief, suffering wrongfully. For what glory is it, if when ye be buffeted for your faults ye shall take it patiently? but if, when ye do well and suffer for it, ye take it patiently, this is acceptable with God."

What happens to the young in one way, and to penitent sinners in another, happens in one way or other to all of us. In the case of all of us occasions arise, when practices countenanced by others do not approve themselves to our consciences. If after serious thought we find we cannot acquiesce in them, we must follow our consciences, and stand prepared for the censure of others. We must submit (should it be unavoidable) to appear to those who have no means of understanding us, self-willed, or self-conceited, or obstinate, or eccentric, or headstrong, praying the while that God's mercy may vouchsafe to us, that we be not really what we seem to the world.

Some are exposed to a temptation of a different kind, that of making themselves seem more religious than they really are. It may happen, that to advocate right opinions may be profitable to our worldly interests, and be attended by the praise of men. You may ask, since in such cases God and man approve the same thing, why should the applause of the world be accounted dangerous then? I answer, it is dangerous because God requires of us a modest silence in our religion; but we cannot be religious in the eyes of men without displaying religion. I am now speaking of display. God sees our thoughts without our help, and praises *them;* but we cannot be praised by men without being seen by men : whereas often the very excellence of a religious action, according to our Saviour's precept, consists in the not being seen by others. This is a frequent cause of hypocrisy in religion. Men begin by feeling as they should feel, then they think it a very hard thing that men should not know how well they feel, and in course of time they learn to speak without feeling. Thus they have learned to " love the praise of men more than the praise of God." —We have to guard against another danger, against the mistake of supposing that the world's despising us is a proof that we are particularly religious; for this, too, is often supposed. Frequently it happens that we encumber our religion with extravagances, perversions, or mistakes, with which religion itself has no necessary connexion, and these, and not religion, excite the contempt of the world. So much is this the case, that the censure of numbers, or of the sober-minded, or of various and distinct classes of men, or censure consistently urged, or continued consistently, ought always to lead a man to be very watchful as to what he considers right to say or do in the line of duty, to lead him to examine his principles; to lead him, however thoroughly he adheres to these after all, to be unaffectedly humble about himself, and to convince him in matter of fact (what he might be quite sure of beforehand, from the nature of the case), that, however good his principles are in themselves, he is mixing up with them the alloy of his own frail and corrupt nature.

In conclusion, I would say to those who fear the world's censure, this :—

1. Recollect you cannot please all parties, you must disagree with some or other: you have only to choose (if you are determined to look to man) with which you will disagree. And, further, you may be sure that those who attempt to please all parties, please fewest; and that the best way to gain the world's good opinion (even if you were set upon this, which you must not be) is to show that you prefer the praise of God. Make up your mind to be occasionally misunderstood, and undeservedly condemned. You must, in the Apostle's words, go through evil report, and good report, whether on a contracted or a wider field of action. And you must not be anxious even for the praise of good men. To have, indeed, the approbation of those whose hearts are guided by God's Holy Spirit, is indeed much to be coveted. Still this is a world of discipline, not of enjoyment ; and just as we are sometimes bound in duty to abstain from indulgences of sense in themselves innocent, so are we sometimes bound to deny ourselves the satisfaction derived from the praise even of the religious and conscientious. Only let us beware in all this, lest we act from pride and self-conceit.

2. In the next place, think of the multitude of beings,

who, unseen themselves, may yet be surveying our conduct. St. Paul charges Timothy by the elect Angels [1]; and elsewhere he declares that the Apostles were made "a spectacle unto the world, and to Angels, and to men [2]." Are we then afraid to follow what is right, lest the world should scoff? rather let us be afraid not to follow it, because God sees us, and Christ, and the holy Angels. They rejoice over one sinner that repenteth; how must they mourn over those who fall away! What interest, surely, is excited among them, by the sight of the Christian's trial, when faith and the desire of the world's esteem are struggling in his heart for victory! what rejoicing if, through the grace of God, he overcomes! what sorrow and pity if he is overcome by the world! Accustom yourselves, then, to feel that you are on a public stage, whatever your station of life may be; that there are other witnesses to your conduct besides the world around you; and, if you feel shame of men, you should much more feel shame in the presence of God, and those servants of His that do His pleasure.

3. Still further: you fear the judgment of men upon you. What will you think of it on your death-bed? The hour must come, sooner or later, when your soul is to return to Him who gave it. Perhaps you will be sensible of your awful state. What will you then think of the esteem of the world? will not all below

[1] 1 Tim. v. 21.　　　　　[2] 1 Cor. iv. 9.

seem to pass away, and be rolled up as a scroll, and the extended regions of the future solemnly set themselves before you? Then how vain will appear the applause or blame of creatures, such as we are, all sinners and blind judges, and feeble aids, and themselves destined to be judged for their deeds. When, then, you are tempted to dread the ridicule of man, throw your mind forward to the hour of death. You know what you will then think of it, if you are then able to think at all.

4. The subject is not exhausted. You fear shame; well, and will you not shrink from shame at the judgment-seat of Christ? There will be assembled all the myriads of men who ever lived, a vast multitude! There will be Apostles, prophets, martyrs, and all saints from the beginning of time. There will be all the good men you ever heard of or knew. There will be your own kindest and best friends, your pious parents, or brothers, or children. Now what think you of being put to shame before all these? You fear the contempt of one small circle of men; what think you of the Saints of God, of St. Mary, of St. Peter and St. Paul, of the ten thousand generations of mankind, being witnesses of your disgrace? You dread the opinion of those whom you do not love; but what if a father then shrink from a dear son, or the wife, or husband, your earthly companion, then tremble at the sight of you, and feel ashamed of you? Nay, there is One greater than parents, husbands, or brothers; One of whom you

have been ashamed on earth; and what will He, that merciful, but neglected Saviour, think of you then? Hear His own words :—" Whosoever shall be ashamed of Me and of My words, of him shall the Son of Man be ashamed, when He shall come in His own glory, and in His Father's, and of the holy Angels." Then such unhappy men, how will they feel shame at themselves! they will despise and loathe themselves; they will hate and abominate their own folly; they will account themselves brutish and mad, so to have been beguiled by the devil, and to have trifled with the season of mercy. " Many of them that sleep in the dust of the earth," says Daniel, " shall awake, some to everlasting life, and some to shame and everlasting contempt."

Let us, then, rouse ourselves, and turn from man to God; what have we to do with the world, who from our infancy have been put on our journey heavenward? Take up your cross and follow Christ. He went through shame far greater than can be yours. Do you think He felt nothing when He was lifted up on the Cross to public gaze, amid the contempt and barbarous triumphings of His enemies, the Pharisees, Pilate and his Roman guard, Herod and his men of war, and the vast multitude collected from all parts of the world? They all looked on Him with hatred and insult; yet He endured (we are told), " despising the shame [1]." It is a high privilege to be allowed to be

[1] Heb. xii. 2.

conformed to Christ; St. Paul thought it so, so have all good men. The whole Church of God, from the days of Christ to the present, has been ever held in shame and contempt by men of this world. Proud men have reasoned against its Divine origin; crafty men have attempted to degrade it to political purposes: still it has lasted for many centuries; it will last still, through the promised help of God the Holy Ghost; and that same promise which is made to it first as a body, is assuredly made also to every one of us who seeks grace from God through it. The grace of our Lord and Saviour is pledged to every one of us without measure, to give us all necessary strength and holiness when we pray for it; and Almighty God tells us Himself, "Fear ye not the reproach of men, neither be ye afraid of their revilings. For the moth shall eat them up like a garment, and the worm shall eat them like wool; but My righteousness shall be for ever, and My salvation from generation to generation."

SERMON V.

TEMPORAL ADVANTAGES.

1 Tim. vi. 7, 8.

" We brought nothing into this world, and it is certain we can carry nothing out. And having food and raiment let us be therewith content."

EVERY age has its own special sins and temptations. Impatience with their lot, murmuring, grudging, unthankfulness, discontent, are sins common to men at all times; but I suppose one of those sins which belongs to our age more than to another, is desire of a greater portion of worldly goods than God has given us,— ambition and covetousness in one shape or another. This is an age and country in which, more than in any other, men have the opportunity of what is called rising in life,—of changing from a lower to a higher class of society, of gaining wealth; and upon wealth all things follow,—consideration, credit, influence, power, enjoyment, the lust of the flesh, and the lust of the eyes, and the pride of life. Since, then, men now-a-days have so often the opportunity of gaining worldly goods which formerly they had not, it is not wonderful they should be tempted to gain them; nor wonderful that when they have gained them, they should set their heart upon them.

And it will often happen, that from coveting them before they are gained, and from making much of them when they are gained, men will be led to take unlawful means, whether to increase them, or not to lose them. But I am not going so far as to suppose the case of dishonesty, fraud, double-dealing, injustice, or the like : to these St. Paul seems to allude when he goes on to say, " They that will be rich fall into temptation and a snare ;" again, " The love of money is the root of all evil." But let us confine ourselves to the consideration of the nature itself, and the natural effects, of these worldly things, without extending our view to those further evils to which they may give occasion. St. Paul says in the text, that we ought to be content with food and raiment; and the wise man says, " Give me neither poverty nor riches ; feed me with food convenient for me[1]." And our Lord would have us " take no thought for the morrow ;" which surely is a dissuasion from aggrandizing ourselves, accumulating wealth, or aiming at distinction. And He has taught us when we pray to say, " Give us this day our *daily* bread." Yet a great number of persons, I may say, nearly all men, are not content with enough, they are

[1] Prov. xxx. 8.

not satisfied with sufficiency; they wish for something
more than simplicity, and plainness, and gravity, and
modesty, in their mode of living; they like show and
splendour, and admiration from the many, and ob-
sequiousness on the part of those who have to do with
them, and the ability to do as they will; they like to
attract the eye, to be received with consideration and
respect, to be heard with deference, to be obeyed with
promptitude; they love greetings in the markets, and
the highest seats; they like to be well dressed, and to
have titles of honour. Now, then, I will attempt to
show that these gifts of the world which men seek are
not to be reckoned good things; that they are ill suited
to our nature and our present state, and are dangerous
to us; that it is on the whole best for our prospects of
happiness even here, not to say hereafter, that we should
be without them.

Now, first, that these worldly advantages, as they are
called, are not productive of any great enjoyment even
now to the persons possessing them, it does not require
many words to prove. I might indeed maintain, with
no slight show of reason, that these things, so far from
increasing happiness, are generally the source of much
disquietude; that as a person has more wealth, or more
power, or more distinction, his cares generally increase,
and his time is less his own : thus, in the words of the
preacher, " the abundance of the rich will not suffer him
to sleep," and, " in much wisdom is much grief, and he

that increaseth knowledge increaseth sorrow[1]." But however this may be, at least these outward advantages do not increase our happiness. Let me ask any one who has succeeded in any object of his desire, has he experienced in his success that full, that lasting satisfaction which he anticipated? Did not some feeling of disappointment, of weariness, of satiety, of disquietude, after a short time, steal over his mind? I think it did; and if so, what reason has he to suppose that that greater share of reputation, opulence, and influence which he has not, and which he desires, would, if granted him, suffice to make him happy? No; the fact is certain, however slow and unwilling we may be to believe it, none of these things bring the pleasure which we beforehand suppose they will bring. Watch narrowly the persons who possess them, and you will at length discover the same uneasiness and occasional restlessness which others have; you will find that there is just a something beyond, which they are striving after, or just some one thing which annoys and distresses them. The good things you admire please for the most part only while they are new; now those who have them are accustomed to them, so they care little for them, and find no alleviation in them of the anxieties and cares which still remain. It is fine, in prospect and imagination, to be looked up to, admired, applauded, courted, feared, to have a name among men,

[1] Eccles. i. 18.

to rule their opinions or their actions by our word, to create a stir by our movements, while men cry, ".Bow the knee," before us; but none knows so well how vain is the world's praise, as he who has it. And why is this? It is, in a word, because the soul was made for religious employments and pleasures; and hence, that no temporal blessings, however exalted or refined, can satisfy it. As well might we attempt to sustain the body on chaff, as to feed and nourish the immortal soul with the pleasures and occupations of the world.

Only thus much, then, shall I say on the point of worldly advantages not bringing present happiness. But next, let us consider that, on the other hand, they are positively dangerous to our eternal interests.

Many of these things, if they did no other harm, at least are injurious to our souls, by taking up the time which might else be given to religion. Much intercourse with the world, which eminence and station render a duty, has a tendency to draw off the mind from God, and deaden it to the force of religious motives and considerations. There is a want of sympathy between much business and calm devotion, great splendour and a simple faith, which will be to no one more painful than to the Christian, to whom God has assigned some post of especial responsibility or distinction. To maintain a religious spirit in the midst of engagements and excitements of this world is possible only to a saint;

nay, the case is the same though our business be one of a charitable and religious nature, and though our chief intercourse is with those whom we believe to have their minds set upon religion, and whose principles and conduct are not likely to withdraw our feet from the narrow way of life. For here we are likely to be deceived from the very circumstance that our employments are religious ; and our end, as being a right one, will engross us, and continually tempt us to be inattentive to the means, and to the spirit in which we pursue it. Our Lord alludes to the danger of multiplied occupations in the Parable of the Sower : " He that received seed among thorns, is he that heareth the word, and the cares of this world and the deceitfulness of riches choke the word, and he becometh unfruitful."

Again, these worldly advantages, as they are called, will seduce us into an excessive love of them. We are too well inclined by nature to live by sight, rather than by faith ; and besides the immediate enjoyment, there is something so agreeable to our natural tastes in the honours and emoluments of the world, that it requires an especially strong mind, and a large measure of grace, not to be gradually corrupted by them. We are led to set our hearts upon them, and in the same degree to withdraw them from God. We become unwilling to leave this visible state of things, and to be reduced to a level with those multitudes who are at present inferior to ourselves. Prosperity is sufficient to seduce, although not to satisfy. Hence death and judgment are unwelcome subjects of reflection to the rich and powerful; for death takes from them those comforts which habit has made necessary to them, and throws them adrift on a new order of things, of which they know nothing, save that in it there is no respect of persons.

And as these goods lead us to love the world, so again do they lead us to trust in the world: we not only become worldly-minded, but unbelieving; our wills becoming corrupt, our understandings also become dark, and disliking the truth, we gradually learn to maintain and defend error. St. Paul speaks of those who "having put away a good conscience, concerning faith made shipwreck[1]." Familiarity with this world makes men discontented with the doctrine of the narrow way; they fall into heresies, and attempt to attain salvation on easier terms than those which Christ holds out to us. In a variety of ways this love of the world operates. Men's opinions are imperceptibly formed by their wishes. If, for instance, we see our worldly prospects depend, humanly speaking, upon a certain person, we are led to court him, to honour him, and adopt his views, and trust in an arm of flesh, till we forget the overruling power of God's providence, and the necessity of His blessing, for the building of the house and the keeping of the city.

[1] 1 Tim. i. 19.

And moreover, these temporal advantages, as they are considered, have a strong tendency to render us self-confident. When a man has been advanced in the world by means of his own industry and skill, when he began poor and ends rich, how apt will he be to pride himself, and confide, in his own contrivances and his own resources! Or when a man feels himself possessed of good abilities; of quickness in entering into a subject, or of powers of argument to discourse readily upon it, or of acuteness to detect fallacies in dispute with little effort, or of a delicate and cultivated taste, so as to separate with precision the correct and beautiful in thought and feeling from the faulty and irregular, how will such an one be tempted to self-complacency and self-approbation! how apt will he be to rely upon himself, to rest contented with himself; to be harsh and impetuous; or supercilious; or to be fastidious, indolent, unpractical; and to despise the pure, self-denying, humble temper of religion, as something irrational, dull, enthusiastic, or needlessly rigorous!

These considerations on the extreme danger of possessing temporal advantages, will be greatly strengthened by considering the conduct of holy men when gifted with them. Take, for instance, Hezekiah, one of the best of the Jewish kings. He, too, had been schooled by occurrences which one might have thought would have beaten down all pride and self-esteem. The king of Assyria had come against him, and seemed prepared to overwhelm him with his hosts; and he had found his God a mighty Deliverer, cutting off in one night of the enemy an hundred fourscore and five thousand men. And again, he had been miraculously recovered from sickness, when the sun's shadow turned ten degrees back, to convince him of the certainty of the promised recovery. Yet when the king of Babylon sent ambassadors to congratulate him on this recovery, we find this holy man ostentatiously displaying to them his silver, and gold, and armour. Truly the heart is "deceitful above all things;" and it was, indeed, to manifest this more fully that God permitted him thus to act. God "left him," says the inspired writer, "to try him, that he might know all that was in his heart[1]." Let us take David as another instance of the great danger of prosperity; he, too, will exemplify the unsatisfactory nature of temporal goods; for which, think you, was the happier, the lowly shepherd or the king of Israel? Observe his simple reliance on God and his composure, when advancing against Goliath: "The Lord," he says, "that delivered me out of the paw of the lion and out of the paw of the bear, He will deliver me out of the hand of this Philistine[2]." And compare this with his grievous sins, his continual errors, his weaknesses, inconsistencies, and then his troubles and mortifications after coming to the throne of Israel; and who will not say that his advancement was the occasion of both sor-

[1] 2 Chron. xxxii. 31.   [2] 1 Sam. xvii. 37.

row and sin, which, humanly speaking, he would have escaped, had he died amid the sheepfolds of Jesse? He was indeed most wonderfully sustained by Divine grace, and died in the fear of God; yet what rightminded and consistent Christian but must shrink from the bare notion of possessing a worldly greatness so corrupting and seducing as David's kingly power was shown to be in the instance of so great a Saint? The case of Solomon is still more striking; his falling away even surpasses our anticipation of what our Saviour calls "the deceitfulness of riches." He may indeed, for what we know, have repented; but at least the history tells us nothing of it. All we are told is, that "King Solomon loved many strange women . . . and it came to pass when Solomon was old, that his wives turned away his heart after other gods; and his heart was not perfect with the Lord his God, as was the heart of David his father. For Solomon went after Ashtaroth, the goddess of the Sidonians, and after Milcom, the abomination of the Ammonites [1]." Yet this was he who had offered up that most sublime and affecting prayer at the Dedication of the Temple, and who, on a former occasion, when the Almighty gave him the choice of any blessing he should ask, had preferred an understanding heart to long life, and honour, and riches.

So dangerous, indeed, is the possession of the goods of this world, that, to judge from the Scripture history,

---

[1] 1 Kings xi. 1. 4, 5.

seldom has God given unmixed prosperity to any one whom He loves. "Blessed is the man," says the Psalmist, "whom Thou chastenest, and teachest him out of Thy law [1]." Even the best men require some pain or grief to sober them and keep their hearts right. Thus, to take the example of St. Paul himself, even his labours, sufferings, and anxieties, he tells us, would not have been sufficient to keep him from being exalted above measure, through the abundance of the revelations, unless there had been added some further cross, some "thorn in the flesh [2]," as he terms it, some secret affliction, of which we are not particularly informed, to humble him, and to keep him in a sense of his weak and dependent condition.

The history of the Church after him affords us an additional lesson of the same serious truth. For three centuries it was exposed to heathen persecution; during that long period God's Hand was upon His people: what did they do when that Hand was taken off? How did they act when the world was thrown open to them, and the saints possessed the high places of the earth? did they enjoy it? far from it, they shrank from that which they might, had they chosen, have made much of; they denied themselves what was set before them; when God's Hand was removed, their own hand was heavy upon them. Wealth, honour, and power, they put away from them. They recollected our Lord's words, "How

---

[1] Ps. xciv. 12.   [2] 2 Cor. xii. 7.

hardly shall they that have riches enter into the kingdom of God [1] !" And St. James's, " Hath not God chosen the poor of this world, rich in faith, and heirs of the kingdom [2]?" For three centuries they had no need to think of those words, for Christ remembered them, and kept them humble; but when He left them to themselves, then they did voluntarily what they had hitherto suffered patiently. They were resolved that the Gospel character of a Christian should be theirs. Still, as before, Christ spoke of His followers as poor and weak, and lowly and simple-minded; men of plain lives, men of prayer, not " faring sumptuously," or clad in " soft raiment," or "taking thought for the morrow." They recollected what He said to the young Ruler, "If thou wilt be perfect, go and sell that thou hast, and give to the poor, and thou shalt have treasure in heaven, and come and follow Me." And so they put off their " gay clothing," their " gold, and pearls, and costly array;" they " sold that they had, and gave alms;" they " washed one another's feet;" they " had all things common." They formed themselves into communities for prayer and praise, for labour and study, for the care of the poor, for mutual edification, and preparation for Christ; and thus, as soon as the world professed to be Christian, Christians at once set up among them a witness against the world, and kings and monks came into the Church together. And from that time to this, never has the union of the

[1] Mark x. 23.   [2] James ii. 5.

Church with the State prospered, but when the Church was in union also with the hermitage and the cell.

Moreover, in those religious ages, Christians avoided greatness in the Church as well as in the world. They would not accept rank and station on account of their spiritual peril, when they were no longer encompassed by temporal trials. When they were elected to the episcopate, when they were appointed to the priesthood, they fled away and hid themselves. They recollected our Lord's words, " Whosoever will be chief among you, let him be your servant;" and again, " Be not ye called Rabbi; for one is your Master, even Christ, and all ye are brethren [1]." And when discovered and forced to the eminence which they shunned, they made much lament, and were in many tears. And they felt that their higher consideration in the world demanded of them some greater strictness and self-denial in their course of life, lest it should turn to a curse, lest the penance of which it would defraud them here, should be visited on them in manifold measure hereafter. They feared to have " their good things " and " their consolation " on earth, lest they should not have Lazarus' portion in heaven. That state of things indeed is now long passed away, but let us not miss the doctrinal lesson which it conveys, if we will not take it for our pattern.

Before I conclude, however, I must take notice of an objection which may be made to what I have been say-

---

[1] Matt. xx. 27; xxiii. 8.

ing. It may be asked, "Are not these dangerous things the gifts of God? Are they not even called blessings? Did not God bestow riches and honour upon Solomon as a reward? And did He not praise him for praying for wisdom? And does not St. Paul say, 'Covet earnestly the best gifts[1]?'" It is true; nor did I ever mean to say that these things were bad in themselves, but bad, for us, if we seek them as ends; and dangerous to us from their fascination. "Every creature of God is good," as St. Paul says, "and nothing to be refused[2];" but circumstances may make good gifts injurious in our particular case. Wine is good in itself, but not for a man in a fever. If our souls were in perfect health, riches and authority, and strong powers of mind, would be very suitable to us: but they are weak and diseased, and require so great a grace of God to bear these advantages well, that we may be well content to be without them.

Still it may be urged, Are we then absolutely to give give them up if we have them, and not accept them when offered? It may be a duty to keep them, it is sometimes a duty to accept them; for in certain cases God calls upon us not so much to put them away, as to put away our old natures, and make us new hearts and new spirits, wherewith to receive them. At the same time, it is merely for our safety to know their perilous nature, and to beware of them, and in no case to take

[1] 1 Cor. xii. 31.   [2] 1 Tim. iv. 4.

them simply for their own sake, but with a view to God's glory. They must be instruments in our hands to promote the cause of Gospel truth. And, in this light, they have their value, and impart their real pleasure; but be it remembered, that value and that happiness are imparted by the end to which they are dedicated; It is "the altar that sanctifieth the gift [1]:" but, compared with the end to which they must be directed, their real and intrinsic excellence is little indeed.

In this point of view it is that we are to covet earnestly the best gifts: for it is a great privilege to be allowed to serve the Church. Have we wealth? let it be the means of extending the knowledge of the truth—abilities? of recommending it—power? of defending it.

From what I have said concerning the danger of possessing the things which the world admires, we may draw the following rule: use them, as far as given, with gratitude for what is really good in them, and with a desire to promote God's glory by means of them; but do not go out of the way to seek them. They will not on the whole make you happier, and they may make you less religious.

For us, indeed, who are all the adopted children of God our Saviour, what addition is wanting to complete our happiness? What can increase their peace who believe and trust in the Son of God? Shall we add a drop to the ocean, or grains to the sand of the sea?

[1] Matt. xxiii. 19.

Shall we ask for an earthly inheritance, who have the fulness of an heavenly one; power, when in prayer we can use the power of Christ; or wisdom, guided as we may be by the true Wisdom and Light of men? It is in this sense that the Gospel of Christ is a leveller of ranks: we pay, indeed, our superiors full reverence, and with cheerfulness as unto the Lord; and we honour eminent talents as deserving admiration and reward; and the more readily act we thus, because these are little things to pay. The time is short; year follows year, and the world is passing away. It is of small consequence to those who are beloved of God, and walk in the Spirit of truth, whether they pay or receive honour, which is but transitory and profitless. To the true Christian the world assumes another and more interesting appearance; it is no longer a stage for the great and noble, for the ambitious to fret in, and the wealthy to revel in; but it is a scene of probation. Every soul is a candidate for immortality. And the more we realize this view of things, the more will the accidental distinctions of nature or fortune die away from our view, and we shall be led habitually to pray, that upon every Christian may descend, in rich abundance, not merely worldly goods, but that heavenly grace which alone can turn this world to good account for us, and make it the path of peace and of life everlasting.

SERMON VI.

THE SEASON OF EPIPHANY.

JOHN ii. 11.

*" This beginning of miracles did Jesus in Cana of Galilee, and mani-
fested forth His glory ; and His disciples believed on Him."*

THE Epiphany is a season especially set apart for
adoring the glory of Christ. The word may be
taken to mean the manifestation of His glory, and leads
us to the contemplation of Him as a King upon His
throne in the midst of His court, with His servants
around Him, and His guards in attendance. At Christ-
mas we commemorate His grace ; and in Lent His
temptation ; and on Good Friday His sufferings and
death ; and on Easter Day His victory ; and on Holy
Thursday His return to the Father ; and in Advent
we anticipate His second coming. And in all of these
seasons He does something, or suffers something : but in
the Epiphany and the weeks after it, we celebrate Him,
not as on His field of battle, or in His solitary retreat,
but as an august and glorious King ; we view Him as
the Object of our worship. Then only, during His

whole earthly history, did He fulfil the type of Solomon, and held (as I may say) a court, and received the homage of His subjects; viz. when He was an infant. His throne was His undefiled Mother's arms; His chamber of state was a cottage or a cave; the worshippers were the wise men of the East, and they brought presents, gold, frankincense, and myrrh. All around and about Him seemed of earth, except to the eye of faith; one note alone had He of Divinity. As great men of this world are often plainly dressed, and look like other men, all but as having some one costly ornament on their breast or on their brow; so the Son of Mary in His lowly dwelling, and in an infant's form, was declared to be the Son of God Most High, the Father of Ages, and the Prince of Peace, by His star; a wonderful appearance which had guided the wise men all the way from the East, even unto Bethlehem.

This being the character of this Sacred Season, our services throughout it, as far as they are proper to it, are full of the image of a king in his royal court, of a sovereign surrounded by subjects, of a glorious prince upon a throne. There is no thought of war, or of strife, or of suffering, or of triumph, or of vengeance connected with the Epiphany, but of august majesty, of power, of prosperity, of splendour, of serenity, of benignity. Now, if at any time, it is fit to say, "The Lord is in His holy temple, let all the earth keep silence before Him[1]."

[1] Hab. ii. 20.

"The Lord sitteth above the waterflood, and the Lord remaineth a king for ever." "The Lord of Hosts is with us; the God of Jacob is our refuge." "O come, let us worship, and fall down, and kneel before the Lord our Maker." "O magnify the Lord our God, and fall down before His footstool, for He is Holy." "O worship the Lord in the beauty of holiness; bring presents, and come into His courts."

I said that at this time of year the portions of our services which are proper to the season are of a character to remind us of a king on his throne, receiving the devotion of his subjects. Such is the narrative itself, already referred to, of the coming of the wise men, who sought Him with their gifts from a place afar off, and fell down and worshipped Him. Such too, is the account of His baptism, which forms the Second Lesson of the feast of the Epiphany, when the Holy Ghost descended on Him, and a Voice from heaven acknowledged Him to be the Son of God. And if we look at the Gospels read throughout the season, we shall find them all containing some kingly action of Christ, the Mediator between God and man. Thus in the Gospel for the First Sunday, He manifests His glory in the temple at the age of twelve years, sitting among the doctors, and astonishing them with His wisdom. In the Gospel for the Second Sunday He manifests His glory at the wedding feast, when He turned the water into wine, a miracle not of necessity or urgency, but especially an august and bountiful act—the act of a King, who out of His abundance gave a gift to His own, therewith to make merry with their friends. In the Third Sunday, the leper worships Christ, who thereupon heals him; the centurion, again, reminds Him of His Angels and ministers, and He speaks the word, and his servant is restored forthwith. In the Fourth, a storm arises on the lake, while He is peacefully sleeping, without care or sorrow, on a pillow; then He rises and rebukes the winds and the sea, and a calm follows, deep as that of His own soul, and the beholders worship Him. And next He casts out Legion, after the man possessed with it had also " run and worshipped Him[1]." In the Fifth, we hear of His kingdom on earth, and of the enemy sowing tares amid the good seed. And in the Sixth, of His second Epiphany from heaven, " with power and great glory."

Such is the series of manifestations which the Sundays after the Epiphany bring before us. When He is with the doctors in the temple, He is manifested as a prophet —in turning the water into wine, as a priest—in His miracles of healing, as a bounteous Lord, giving out of His abundance—in His rebuking the sea, as a Sovereign, whose word is law—in the parable of the wheat and tares, as a guardian and ruler—in His second coming, as a lawgiver and judge.

And as in these Gospels we hear of our Saviour's

[1] Mark v. 6.

greatness, so in the Epistles and First Lessons we hear of the privileges and the duties of the new people, whom He has formed to show forth His praise.   Christians are at once the temple of Christ, and His worshippers and ministers *in* the temple; they are the Bride of the Lamb taken collectively, and taken individually, they are the friends of the Bridegroom and the guests at the marriage feast.   In these various points of view are they presented to us in the Services during these weeks. In the Lessons from the prophet Isaiah we read of the gifts and privileges, the characteristics, the power, the fortunes of the Church—how widely spreading, even throughout all the Gentiles; how awful and high, how miraculously endowed, how revered, how powerful upon earth, how rich in temporal goods, how holy, how pure in doctrine, how full of the Spirit.   And in the Epistles for the successive Sundays, we hear of the duties and distinguishing marks of her true members, principally as laid down in the twelfth and thirteenth chapters of St. Paul to the Romans; then as the same Apostle enjoins them upon the Colossians; and then in St. John's exhortations in his General Epistle.

The Collects are of the same character, as befit the supplications of subjects coming before their King. The first is for knowledge and power, the second is for peace, the third is for strength in our infirmities, the fourth is for help in temptation, the fifth is for protection, and the sixth is for preparation and purification against Christ's second coming. There is none which would suit a season of trial, or of repentance, or of waiting, or of exultation—they befit a season of peace, thanksgiving, and adoration, when Christ is not manifested in pain, conflict, or victory, but in the tranquil possession of His kingdom.

It will be sufficient to make one reflection, which suggests itself from what I have been saying.

You will observe, then, that the only display of royal greatness, the only season of majesty, homage, and glory, which our Lord had on earth, was in His infancy and youth. Gabriel's message to Mary was in its style and manner such as befitted an Angel speaking to Christ's Mother. Elisabeth, too, saluted Mary, and the future Baptist his hidden Lord, in the same honourable way. Angels announced His birth, and the shepherds worshipped. A star appeared, and the wise men rose from the East and made Him offerings. He was brought to the temple, and Simeon took Him in His arms, and returned thanks for Him. He grew to twelve years old, and again He appeared in the temple, and took His seat in the midst of the doctors. But here His earthly majesty had its end, or if seen afterwards, it was but now and then, by glimpses and by sudden gleams, but with no steady sustained light, and no diffused radiance. We are told at the close of the last-mentioned narrative, "And He went down with His parents, and came to Nazareth, *and was subjected unto them*[1]." His subjection and servitude now began in fact. He had come in the form of a servant, and now He took on Him a servant's office. How much is contained in the idea of His subjection! and it began, and His time of glory ended, when He was twelve years old.

Solomon, the great type of the Prince of Peace, reigned forty years, and his name and greatness was known far and wide through the East. Joseph, the much-loved son of Jacob, who in an earlier age of the Church, was a type of Christ in His kingdom, was in power and favour eighty years, twice as long as Solomon. But Christ, the true Revealer of secrets, and the Dispenser of the bread of life, the true wisdom and majesty of the Father, manifested His glory but in His early years, and then the Sun of Righteousness was clouded. For He was not to reign really, till He left the world. He has reigned ever since; nay, reigned *in* the world, though He is not in sensible presence in it—the invisible King of a visible kingdom—for He came on earth but to show what His reign would be, after He had left it, and to submit to suffering and dishonour, that He *might* reign.

It often happens, that when persons are in serious illnesses, and in delirium in consequence, or other disturbance of mind, they have some few minutes of respite in the midst of it, when they are even more than them-

[1] Luke ii. 51.

selves, as if to show us what they really are, and to interpret for us what else would be dreary. And again, some have thought that the minds of children have on them traces of something more than earthly, which fade away as life goes on, but are the promise of what is intended for them hereafter. And somewhat in this way, if we may dare compare ourselves with our gracious Lord, in a parallel though higher way, Christ descends to the shadows of this world, with the transitory tokens on Him of that future glory into which He could not enter till He had suffered. The star burned brightly over Him for awhile, though it then faded away.

We see the same law, as it may be called, of Divine Providence in other cases also. Consider, for instance, how the prospect of our Lord's passion opens upon the Apostles in the sacred history. Where did they hear of it? "Moses and Elias on the mountain appeared with Him in glory, and spake of His decease, which He should accomplish at Jerusalem [1]." That is, the season of His bitter trial was preceded by a short gleam of the glory which was to be, when He was suddenly transfigured, "and the fashion of His countenance was altered, and His raiment was white and glistering [2]." And with this glory in prospect, our Lord abhorred not to die: as it is written, "Who for the joy that was set before Him, endured the Cross, despising the shame."

Again, He forewarned His Apostles that they in like

---

[1] Luke ix. 30, 31.　　　　　　　　[2] Luke ix. 29.

manner should be persecuted for righteousness' sake, and be afflicted and delivered up, and hated and killed. Such was to be their life in this world, "that if in this world only they had had hope in Christ, they had been of all men most miserable[1]." Well then, observe, their trial too was preceded by a season of peace and pleasantness, in anticipation of their future reward; for before the day of Pentecost, for forty days Christ was with them, soothing, comforting, confirming them, "and speaking of the things pertaining unto the kingdom of God[2]." As Moses stood on the mount and saw the promised land and all its riches, and yet Joshua had to fight many battles before he got possession, so did the Apostles, before descending into the valley of the shadow of death, whence nought of heaven was to be seen, stand upon the heights, and look over that valley, which they had to cross, to the city of the living God beyond it.

And so again, St. Paul, after many years of toil, refers back to a time when he had a celestial vision, anticipatory of what was to be his blessedness in the end. "I knew a man in Christ," he says, meaning himself, "about fourteen years ago, caught up to the third heaven. . . . And I knew such a man . . . how that he was caught up into Paradise, and heard unspeakable words, which it is not lawful for a man to utter[3]." St. Paul then, as the twelve Apostles, and as our Lord before

[1] 1 Cor. xv. 19.   [2] Acts i. 3.   [3] 2 Cor. xii. 3, 4.

him, had his brief season of repose and consolation before the battle.

And lastly : the whole Church also may be said to have had a similar mercy vouchsafed to it at first, in anticipation of what is to be in the end. We know, alas, too well, that, according to our Lord's account of it, tares are to be with the wheat, fish of every kind in the net, all through its sojourning on earth. But in the end, " the saints shall stand before the throne of God, and serve Him day and night in His temple : and the Lamb shall feed them, and shall lead them unto living fountains of waters," and there shall be no more " sorrow nor pain, nor any thing that defileth or worketh abomination," " for without are dogs, and sorcerers, and whoremongers, and murderers, and idolaters, and whosoever loveth and maketh a lie." Now was not this future glory shadowed forth in that infancy of the Church, when before the seal of the new dispensation was opened and trial began, " there was silence in heaven for half an hour;" and " the disciples continued daily with one accord in the temple, and in prayers, breaking bread from house to house, being of one heart, and of one soul, eating their meat with gladness and singleness of heart, praising God, and having favour with all the people [1];" while hypocrites and " liars," like Ananias and Sapphira, were struck dead, and " sorcerers," like Simon, were detected and denounced ?

[1] Acts ii. 46, 47.

To conclude; let us thankfully cherish all seasons of peace and joy which are vouchsafed us here below. Let us beware of abusing them, and of resting in them, of forgetting that they *are* special privileges, of neglecting to look out for trouble and trial, as our due and our portion. Trial is our portion here—we must not think it strange when trial comes after peace. Still God mercifully does grant a respite now and then; and perhaps He grants it to us the more, the more careful we are not to abuse it. For all seasons we must thank Him, for time of sorrow and time of joy, time of warfare and time of peace. And the more we thank Him for the one, the more we shall be drawn to thank Him for the other. Each has its own proper fruit, and its own peculiar blessedness. Yet our mortal flesh shrinks from the one, and of itself prefers the other;—it prefers rest to toil, peace to war, joy to sorrow, health to pain and sickness. When then Christ gives us what is pleasant, let us take it as a refreshment by the way, that we may, when God calls, go in the strength of that meat forty days and forty nights unto Horeb, the mount of God. Let us rejoice in Epiphany with trembling, that at Septuagesima we may go into the vineyard with the labourers with cheerfulness, and may sorrow in Lent with thankfulness; let us rejoice now, not as if we have attained, but in hope of attaining. Let us take our present happiness, not as our true rest, but, as what the land of Canaan was to the Israelites,—a type and shadow of it. If we now enjoy God's ordinances, let us not cease to pray that they may prepare us for His presence hereafter. If we enjoy the presence of friends, let them remind us of the communion of saints before His throne. Let us trust in nothing here, yet draw hope from every thing—that at length the Lord may be our everlasting light, and the days of our mourning may be ended.

SERMON VII.

THE DUTY OF SELF-DENIAL.

PSALM cxxxi. 2.

" Surely I have behaved and quieted myself, as a child that is weaned of his mother : my soul is even as a weaned child."

SELF-DENIAL of some kind or other is involved, as is evident, in the very notion of renewal and holy obedience. To change our hearts is to learn to love things which we do not naturally love—to unlearn the love of this world; but this involves, of course, a thwarting of our natural wishes and tastes. To be righteous and obedient implies self-command; but to possess power we must have gained it; nor can we gain it without a vigorous struggle, a persevering warfare against ourselves. The very notion of being religious implies self-denial, because by nature we do not love religion.

Self-denial, then, is a subject never out of place in Christian teaching; still more appropriate is it at a time like this, when we have entered upon the forty days of Lent, the season of the year set apart for fasting and humiliation.

This indeed is not all that is meant by self-denial; but before proceeding with the subject, I would ask whether the generality of mankind go as far as this: it is plain that they do not. They do not go so far as to realize to themselves that religious obedience involves a thwarting of those wishes and inclinations which are natural to them. They do not like to be convinced, much less will they act upon the notion, that religion is difficult. You may hear men of the world say plainly, and as if in the way of argument, "that God will not punish us for indulging the passions with which we are born; that it is no praise to be unnatural; and no crime to be a man." This, however, may seem an extreme case; yet are there not a great many decent and respectable men, as far as outward character goes, who at least fix their thoughts on worldly comfort, as the greatest of goods, and who labour to place themselves in easy circumstances, under the notion that, when they can retire from the business of their temporal calling, then they may (in a quiet, unexceptionable way of course) consult their own tastes and likings, take their pleasure, and indulge themselves in self-importance and self-satisfaction, in the enjoyment of wealth, power, distinction, popularity, and credit? I am not at this moment asking whether such indulgences are in themselves allowable or not, but whether the life which centres in them does not imply the absence of any very deep views of sanctification as a process, a change, a painful toil, of working out our own salvation with fear and trembling, of preparing to meet our God, and waiting for the judgment? You may go into mixed society; you will hear men conversing on their friend's prospects, openings in trade, or realized wealth, on his advantageous situation, the pleasant connexions he has formed, the land he has purchased, the house he has built; then they amuse themselves with conjecturing what this or that man's property may be, where he lost, where he gained, his shrewdness, or his rashness, or his good fortune in this or that speculation. Observe, I do not say that such conversation is wrong; I do not say that we must always have on our lips the very thoughts which are deepest in our hearts, or that it is safe to judge of individuals by such speeches; but when this sort of conversation is the customary standard conversation of the world, and when a line of conduct answering to it is the prevalent conduct of the world (and this is the case), is it not a grave question for each of us, as living in the world, to ask himself what abiding notion we have of the necessity of self-denial, and how far we are clear of the danger of resembling that evil generation which "ate and drank, which married wives, and were given in marriage, which bought and sold, planted, and builded, till it rained fire and brimstone from heaven, and destroyed them all [1] ?"

It is strange, indeed, how far this same forgetfulness

[1] Luke xvii. 27—29.

and transgression of the duty of self-denial at present spreads. Take another class of persons, very different from those just mentioned, men who profess much love for religion—I mean such as maintain, that if a man has faith he will have works without his trouble, so that he need be at no pains about performing them. Such persons at best seem to say, that religious obedience is to follow as a matter of course, an easy work, or rather a necessary consequence, from having some strong urgent motive, or from some bright vision of the Truth acting on the mind; and thus they dismiss from their religion the notion of self-denial, or the effort and warfare of faith against our corrupt natural will, whether they actually own that they dismiss it or not. I say that they do this at best; for it often happens, as I just now intimated, that they actually avow their belief that faith is all-sufficient, and do not let their minds dwell at all on the necessity of works of righteousness. All this being considered, surely I am not wrong in saying that the notion of self-denial as a distinct religious duty, and, much more (as it may well be called), the essence of religious obedience, is not admitted into the minds of the generality of men.

But let it be observed, I have hitherto spoken of self-denial not as a distinct duty actually commanded in Scripture, but merely as it is involved in the very notion of sanctification, as necessarily attendant on that change of nature which God the Holy Spirit vouchsafes to work within us. But now let us consider it in the light of the Scripture precepts concerning it, and we shall come to a still more serious view of it, serious (I mean) to those who are living to the world; it is this,—that it is our duty, not only to deny ourselves in what is sinful, but even, in a certain measure, in lawful things, to keep a restraint over ourselves even in innocent pleasures and enjoyments.

Now the first proof I shall give of this will at the same time explain what I mean.

Fasting is clearly a Christian duty, as our Saviour implies in His Sermon on the Mount. Now what is fasting but a refraining from what is lawful; not merely from what is sinful, but what is innocent?—from that bread which we might lawfully take and eat with thanksgiving, but which at certain times we do not take, in order to deny ourselves. Such is Christian self-denial,— not merely a mortification of what is sinful, but an abstinence even from God's blessings.

Again : consider the following declaration of our Saviour : He first tells us, "Strait is the gate, and narrow is the way which leadeth unto life, and few there be that find it." And again : "Strive to enter in, for many, I say unto you, will seek (only seek) to enter in, and shall not be able." Then He explains to us what this peculiar difficulty of a Christian's life consists in : "If any man come to Me, and hate not his father, and mother, and wife, and children, and brethren, and sisters, yea, and his own life also, he cannot be My disciple[1]." Now whatever is precisely meant by this (which I will not here stop to inquire), so far is evident, that our Lord enjoins a certain refraining, not merely from sin, but from innocent comforts and enjoyments of this life, or a self-denial in things lawful.

Again, He says, " If any man will come after Me, let him deny himself, and take up his cross daily, and follow Me[2]." Here He shows us from His own example what Christian self-denial is. It is taking on us a cross after His pattern, not a mere refraining from sin, for He had no sin, but a giving up what we might lawfully use. This was the peculiar character in which Christ came on earth. It was this spontaneous and exuberant self-denial which brought Him down. He who was one with God, took upon Him our nature, and suffered death—and why? to save us whom He needed not save. Thus He denied Himself, and took up His cross. This is the very aspect, in which God, as revealed in Scripture, is distinguished from that exhibition of His glory, which nature gives us: power, wisdom, love, mercy, long-suffering—these attributes, though far more fully and clearly displayed in Scripture than in nature, still are in their degree seen on the face of the visible creation; but self-denial, if it may be said, this incomprehensible attribute of Divine Providence, is disclosed to us only in Scripture. " God so loved the world that

---

[1] Matt. vii. 14. Luke xiii. 24; xiv. 26.   [2] Luke ix. 23.

He gave His Son [1]." Here is self-denial. And the Son of God so loved us, that "though He was rich yet for our sakes He became poor [2]." Here is our Saviour's self-denial. "He pleased not Himself."

And what Christ did when He came on earth, that have all His saints done both before and since His coming. Even the saints of the Old Testament so conducted themselves, to whom a temporal promise was made, and who, if any, might have surrendered themselves to the enjoyment of it. They had a temporal promise, they had a present reward; yet, with a noble faith, and a largeness of soul (how they put us to shame who have so much higher privileges!) the Jewish believers grudged themselves the milk and honey of Canaan, as seeking a better country, that is a heavenly. Elijah, how unlike is he to one who had a temporal promise! Or take again the instance of Daniel, which is still more striking,—"They that wear soft clothing are in kings' houses." Daniel was first in power in the palace of the greatest monarchs of his time. Yet what do we read of him? First of his living upon pulse and water, afterwards of his fasting in sackcloth and ashes, at another time of his mourning three full weeks, eating no pleasant bread, neither flesh nor wine coming in his mouth, nor anointing himself at all, till those three weeks were fulfilled. Can any thing more clearly show the duty of self-denial, even in lawful things, in the

[1] John iii. 16.   [2] 2 Cor. viii. 9.

case of Christians, when even God's servants, before Christ came and commanded it, in proportion as they had evangelical gifts, observed it?

Or again, consider the words of the text spoken by David, who, if any, had riches and power poured upon him by the hand of God. He says, he has "behaved and quieted" himself lest he should be proud, and made himself "as a weaned child." What an impressive word is "weaned!" David had put away the unreserved love and the use of this world. We naturally love the world, and innocently; it is before us, and meets our eyes and hands first; its pleasures are dear to us, and many of them not in themselves sinful, only in their excess, and some of them not sinful at all;—those, for instance, which we derive from our home, our friends, and our prospects, are the first and natural food of our mind. But as children are weaned from their first nourishment, so must our souls put away childish things, and be turned from the pleasures of earth to those of heaven; we must learn to compose and quiet ourselves as a weaned child, to put up with the loss of what is dear to us, nay, voluntarily to give it up for Christ's sake.

Much more after Christ came does St. Paul give us this same lesson in the ninth chapter of his first Epistle to the Corinthians: "Every one that striveth for the mastery is temperate in all things," i. e. has power over himself, and keeps himself in subjection, as he presently says. Again, in the seventh chapter, " The time is short ; it remaineth that both they that have wives be as though they had none, and they that weep as though they wept not, and they that rejoice as though they rejoiced not, and they that buy as though they possessed not, and they that use this world as not abusing it." Here the same doctrine of moderation or temperance in lawful indulgences is strongly enforced ; to weep, to rejoice, to buy, to possess, to marry, to use this world, are not unlawful, yet we must not use God's earthly gifts to the full, but in all things we must be self-denying.

Such is Christian self-denial, and it is incumbent upon us for many reasons. The Christian denies himself in things lawful because he is aware of his own weakness and liability to sin ; he dares not walk on the edge of a precipice ; instead of going to the extreme of what is allowable, he keeps at a distance from evil, that he may be safe. He abstains lest he should not be temperate ; he fasts lest he should eat and drink with the drunken. As is evident, many things are in themselves right and unexceptionable which are inexpedient in the case of a weak and sinful creature : his case is like that of a sick person ; many kinds of food, good for a man in health, are hurtful when he is ill—wine is poison to a man in a fierce fever. And just so, many acts, thoughts, and feelings, which would have been allowable in Adam before his fall, are prejudicial or dangerous in man fallen. For instance, anger is not sinful in itself. St. Paul implies this, when he says, " Be ye angry and sin not [1]." And our Saviour on one occasion is said to have been angry, and He was sinless. Almighty God, too, is angry with the wicked. Anger, then, is not in itself a sinful feeling; but in man, constituted as he is, it is so highly dangerous to indulge it, that self-denial here is a duty from mere prudence. It is almost impossible for a man to be angry only so far as he ought to be ; he will exceed the right limit ; his anger will degenerate into pride, sullenness, malice, cruelty, revenge, and hatred. It will inflame his diseased soul, and poison it. Therefore, he must abstain from it, as if it were *in itself* a sin (though it is not), for it is practically such to him.

Again, the love of praise is in itself an innocent passion, and might be indulged, were the world's opinion right and our hearts sound ; but, as things are, human applause, if listened to, will soon make us forget how weak and sinful we are ; so we must deny ourselves, and accept the praise even of good men, and those we love, cautiously and with reserve.

So, again, love of power is commonly attendant on a great mind ; but he is the greatest of a sinful race who refrains himself, and turns from the temptation of it ; for it is at once unbecoming and dangerous in a son of Adam. " Whosoever will be great among you, let him be your minister," says our Lord ; " and whosoever will

[1] Eph. iv. 26.

be chief among you, let him be your servant[1]." His reward will be hereafter; to reign with Christ, to sit down with Him on His throne, to judge angels,—yet without pride.

Again, even in affection towards our relations and friends, we must be watchful over ourselves, lest it seduce us from the path of duty. Many a father, from a kind wish to provide well for his family, neglects his own soul. Here, then, is a fault; not that we can love our relations too well, but that that strong and most praiseworthy affection for them may, accidentally, ensnare and corrupt our weak nature.

These considerations will show us the meaning of our Saviour's words already cited, about the duty of hating our friends. To hate is to feel that perfect [distaste for an object, that you wish it put away and got rid of; it is to turn away from it, and to blot out the thought of it from your mind. Now this is just the feeling we must cherish towards all earthly blessings, so far as Christ does not cast His light upon them. He (blessed be His name) has sanctioned and enjoined love and care for our relations and friends. Such love is a great duty; but should at any time His guidance lead us by a strange way, and the light of His providence pass on, and cast these objects of our earthly affection into the shade, then they must be at once in the shade to *us*,—they must, for the time, disappear from our hearts. " He that

---

[1] Matt. xx. 26, 27.

loveth father or mother more than Me, is not worthy of Me." So He says; and at such times, though still loving them, we shall seem to hate them; for we shall put aside the thought of them, and act as if they did not exist. And in this sense an ancient and harsh proverb is true : we must always so love our friends as feeling that one day or other we may perchance be called upon to hate them,—that is, forget them in the pursuit of higher duties.

Here, again, then, is an instance of self-denial in lawful things; and if a person says it is painful thus to feel, and that it checks the spontaneous and continual flow of love towards our friends to have this memento sounding in our ears, we must boldly acknowledge that it *is* painful. It is a sad thought, not that we can ever be called upon actually to put away the love of them, but to have to act as if we did not love them,—as Abraham when called on to slay his son. And this thought of the uncertainty of the future, doubtless, does tinge all our brightest affections (as far as this world is concerned) with a grave and melancholy hue. We need not shrink from this confession, remembering that this life is not our rest or happiness;—"*that* remaineth" to come. This sober chastised feeling is the very temper of David, when he speaks of having composed and quieted his soul, and weaned it from the babe's nourishment which this world supplies.

I hope I have made it clear, by these instances, what

[VII]   H is meant by Christian self-denial. If we have good health, and are in easy circumstances, let us beware of high-mindedness, self-sufficiency, self-conceit, arrogance; of delicacy of living, indulgences, luxuries, comforts. Nothing is so likely to corrupt our hearts, and to seduce us from God, as to surround ourselves with comforts,—to have things our own way,—to be the centre of a sort of world, whether of things animate or inanimate, which minister to us. For then, in turn, we shall depend on them; they will become necessary to us; their very service and adulation will lead us to trust ourselves to them, and to idolize them. What examples are there in Scripture of soft luxurious men! Was it Abraham before the Law, who wandered through his days, without a home? or Moses, who gave the Law, and died in the wilderness? or David under the Law, who "had no proud looks," and was "as a weaned child?" or the Prophets, in the latter days of the Law, who wandered in sheep-skins and goat-skins? or the Baptist, when the Gospel was superseding it, who was clad in raiment of camel's hair, and ate the food of the wilderness? or the Apostles, who were "the offscouring of all things"? or our blessed Saviour, who "had not a place to lay His head"? Who are the soft luxurious men in Scripture? There was the rich man, who "fared sumptuously every day," and then "lifted up his eyes in hell, being in torments." There was that other, whose "ground brought forth plentifully," and who said, "Soul, thou hast much goods laid up for many years;" and his soul was required of him that night. There was Demas, who forsook St. Paul, "having loved this present world." And, alas! there was that highly-favoured, that divinely-inspired king, rich and wise Solomon, whom it availed nothing to have measured the earth, and numbered its inhabitants, when in his old age he "loved many strange women," and worshipped their gods.

Far be it from us, soldiers of Christ, thus to perplex ourselves with this world, who are making our way towards the world to come. "No man that warreth, entangleth himself with the affairs of this life, that he may please Him who hath chosen him to be a soldier. If a man also strive for masteries, yet is he not crowned, except he strive lawfully." This is St. Paul's rule, as has already been referred to: accordingly, in another place, he bears witness of himself that he "died daily." Day by day he got more and more dead to this world; he had fewer ties to earth, a larger treasure in heaven. Nor let us think that it is over-difficult to imitate him, though we be not Apostles, nor are called to any extraordinary work, nor are enriched with any miraculous gifts: he would have all men like himself, and all may be like him, according to their place and measure of grace. If we would be followers of the great Apostle, first let us with him fix our eyes upon Christ our Saviour; consider the splendour and glory of His holiness, and

try to love it. Let us strive and pray that the love of
holiness may be created within our hearts; and then acts
will follow, such as befit us and our circumstances, in due
time, without our distressing ourselves to find what they
should be. You need not attempt to draw any precise
line between what is sinful and what is only allowable:
look up to Christ, and deny yourselves every thing,
whatever its character, which you think He would have
you relinquish. You need not calculate and measure, if
you love much: you need not perplex yourselves with
points of curiosity, if you have a heart to venture after
Him. True, difficulties will sometimes arise, but they
will be seldom. He bids you take up your cross; therefore accept the daily opportunities which occur of yield-
ing to others, when you need not yield, and of doing
unpleasant services, which you might avoid. He bids
those who would be highest, live as the lowest: therefore, turn from ambitious thoughts, and (as far as you
religiously may) make resolves against taking on you
authority and rule. He bids you sell and give alms;
therefore, hate to spend money on yourself. Shut your
ears to praise, when it grows loud: set your face like a
flint, when the world ridicules, and smile at its threats.
Learn to master your heart, when it would burst forth
into vehemence, or prolong a barren sorrow, or dissolve
into unseasonable tenderness. Curb your tongue, and
turn away your eye, lest you fall into temptation. Avoid
the dangerous air which relaxes you, and brace yourself

upon the heights. Be up at prayer "a great while before day," and seek the true, your only Bridegroom, "by night on your bed." So shall self-denial become natural to you, and a change come over you, gently and imperceptibly; and, like Jacob, you will lie down in the waste, and will soon see Angels, and a way opened for you into heaven.

SERMON VIII.

THE YOKE OF CHRIST.

MATT. xi. 29, 30.

"Take My yoke upon you, and learn of Me, for I am meek and lowly in heart, and ye shall find rest unto your souls; for My yoke is easy, and My burden is light."

THESE words, which are brought before us in the Gospel of to-day's festival [1], are also found in the address made to us upon Ash Wednesday, in which we are told that if we "return unto Him who is the merciful Receiver of all true penitent sinners, if we will take His easy yoke and light burden upon us, to follow Him in lowliness, patience, and charity; this, if we do, Christ will deliver us from the curse of the law, and from the extreme malediction which shall light upon them that shall be set on the left hand." A few days since we were upon a Fast-day called to take on us Christ's yoke, and now on a Festival of an Apostle the call is repeated.

[1] Preached on St. Matthias's day during Lent.

And with a particular fitness it occurs, now as often, that we celebrate the feast of St. Matthias, during Lent; for if there be an Apostle who above the rest may be taken to remind us of the duty of mortification, it is he. Our Lord, when asked why His disciples did not fast, said, they could not fast while He was with them, but that the time would come, when the Bridegroom should be taken away from them, and then should they fast in those days. That time was now come, when St. Matthias was chosen to be an Apostle. Christ *had* gone away. Peace and joy the Apostles had abundantly, more so than when He was with them; but for that very reason, it was not such a joy " as the world giveth." It was His own joy which arose out of pain and chastisement. This was the joy which St. Matthias received when he was made an Apostle. He never had been an Apostle under age. He had indeed been with our Lord, but not as an Apostle. The rest had been chosen (as it were) as children; they had been heirs of the kingdom, while under tutors and governors, and, though Apostles, had not understood their calling; had had ambitious thoughts or desires after riches, and were indulged for a while, ere new made, with the old wine, lest the bottles should burst. But St. Matthias came into his inheritance at once. He took upon him at once, upon his election, the power and the penalty of the Apostolate. No dreams of earthly prosperity could flit around that throne, which was reared over the grave of one who had been tried and had fallen, and under the immediate shadow of the cross of Him whom he had betrayed.

Well, then, does St. Matthias repeat to us on this day our Lord's words, " Take My yoke upon you, and learn of Me," for he had taken it on him from the first. His Pastoral Staff had ever been a crosier. He had had no youth. He had borne the yoke in his youth. He entered at once upon his long Lent, and he rejoiced in it.

The exhortation, then, which our Saviour gives in to-day's Gospel, and of which St. Matthias's history reminds us, is at the present season most suitable. Our Saviour says, " Come unto Me," and then He adds, " Take My yoke upon you, and learn of Me." Thus He first calls us to Him, and next shows us the way. " Come unto Me," He says, " and I will give you rest;" and then adds, "Take My yoke upon you, and ye shall find rest for your souls." He told the Apostles that they must come to Him, but did not at once tell them the way; He told them they must bear a yoke, but did not at once tell them what it was. St. Peter, in consequence, inquired about it on one occasion, and was bid to wait awhile, and he should know of it more plainly. Our Lord had said, " Whither I go, thou canst not follow Me now, but thou shalt follow Me afterwards." " Ye shall seek Me," He said, " and whither I go ye cannot come¹."

¹ John xiii. 36. 33.

He spoke of His yoke, the way of His cross, as St. Peter found when at length, after His resurrection, he was told plainly what should befall him. "When thou wast young," said our Lord to him, by the lake of Tiberias, when thou wast a child in the faith, and hadst thine own way, "thou girdedst thyself, and walkedst whither thou wouldest," as just before St. Peter had girt his fisher's coat unto him, and cast himself into the sea; "but when thou shalt be old, thou shalt stretch forth thy hands, and another shall gird thee, and carry thee whither thou wouldest not [1]." And then He added, "Follow Me." St. Peter, indeed, was called upon literally to take Christ's yoke upon him, to learn of Him and walk in His ways; but what he underwent in fulness, all Christ's disciples must share in their measure, in some way or other. Again, in another place, our Lord speaks more expressly; "If any man will come after Me, let him deny himself, and take up his cross, and follow Me [2]." Here we have the words of the text emphatically repeated. To come to Christ, is to come after Him; to take up our cross, is to take upon us His yoke; and though He calls this an easy yoke, yet it is easy because it is His yoke, and He makes it easy; still it does not cease to be a yoke, and it is troublesome and distressing, because it is a yoke.

Let us set it down then, as a first principle in reli-

[1] John xxi. 18. [2] Matt. xvi. 24.

gion, that all of us must come to Christ, in some sense or other, through things naturally unpleasant to us; it may be even through bodily suffering, such as the Apostles endured, or it may be nothing more than the subduing of our natural infirmities and the sacrifice of our natural wishes; it may be pain greater or pain less, on a public stage or a private one; but, till the words "yoke" and "cross" can stand for something pleasant, the bearing of our yoke and cross is something not pleasant; and though rest is promised as our reward, yet the way to rest must lie through discomfort and distress of heart.

This I say must be taken as a first principle in religion; it concerns us all, it concerns young and old, rich and poor, all of whom are apt to consider it a valid reason for disregarding and speaking against a religious life, that it is so strict and distasteful. They shrink from religion as something gloomy, or frightful, or dull, or intrusive, or exorbitant. And, alas, sometimes it is attempted to lead them to religion by making it appear not difficult and severe. Severe truths are put aside; religion is made to consist in a worldly security, or again in a heated enthusiastic state of mind. But this is a deceit. I do not of course mean, far from it, that religion is not full of joy and peace also; "My yoke," says Christ, "is easy, and My burden is light:" but grace makes it so; in itself it is severe, and any form of doctrine which teaches otherwise forgets that

Christ calls us to His yoke, and that that yoke is a cross.

If you call to mind some of the traits of that special religious character to which we are called, you will readily understand how both it, and the discipline by which it is formed in us, are not naturally pleasant to us. That character is described in the text as meekness and lowliness; for we are told to " learn" of Him who was " meek and lowly in heart." The same character is presented to us at greater length in our Saviour's sermon on the Mount, in which seven notes of a Christian are given to us, in themselves of a painful and humbling character, but joyful, because they are blessed by Him. He mentions, first, " the poor in spirit;" this is denoted in the text, under the word " lowly in heart;"—secondly, those " that mourn;" and this surely is their peculiarity who are bearing on their shoulders the yoke of Christ;—thirdly, " the meek;" and these too are spoken of in the text, when He bids us to be like Himself who " is meek;"—fourthly, those which do " hunger and thirst after righteousness;" and what righteousness, but that which Christ's Cross wrought out, and which becomes our righteousness when we take on us the yoke of the Cross? Fifthly, " the merciful;" and as the Cross is in itself the work of infinite mercy, so when we bear it, it makes us merciful. Sixthly, " the pure in heart;" and this is the very benefit which the Cross first does to us when marked on our forehead when infants, to sever us from the world, the flesh, and the devil, to circumcise us from the first Adam, and to make us pure as He is pure. Seventhly, "the peace-makers," and as He "made peace by the blood of His Cross," so do we become peace-makers after His pattern. And, lastly, after all seven, He adds, those "which are persecuted for righteousness' sake;" which is nothing but the Cross itself, and the truest form of His yoke, spoken of last of all, after mention has been made of its fruits.

Such is the character of which the text speaks. A man who is poor in spirit, meek, pure in heart, merciful, peace-making, penitent, and eager after righteousness, is truly (according to a term in current use) a mortified man. He is of a character which does not please us by nature even to see, and much less to imitate. We do not even approve or love the character itself, till we have some portion of the grace of God. We do not like the look of mortification till we are used to it, and associate pleasant thoughts with it. "And when we shall see Him, there is no beauty, that we should desire Him," says the Prophet. To whom has some picture of saint or doctor of the Church any charm at first sight? Who does not prefer the ruddy glow of health and brightness of the eyes? "He hath no form nor comeliness," as his Lord and Master before him. And as we do not like the look of saintliness, neither do we like the life. When Christ first announced His destined sufferings, Peter took Him and began to rebuke Him, saying, "Be it far from Thee, Lord, this shall not be unto Thee." Here was the feeling of one who was as yet a mere child in grace; "When he was a child, he spake as a child, he understood as a child, he thought as a child," before he had "become a man and had put away childish things."

This is St. Paul's language, writing to the Corinthians, and he there furnishes us with another description, under the name of charity, of that same heavenly temper of mind in which Christian manhood consists, and which our Lord had already described in the sermon on the Mount; He says, "Though I speak with the tongues of men and of angels, and have not charity, I am become as sounding brass, or a tinkling cymbal." And then He describes it as suffering long, kind, envying not, vaunting not, behaving seemly, unselfish, rejoicing in the truth, slow to be provoked, bearing all things and hoping all. And with this agrees St. James's account of wisdom, that it is "pure, peaceable, gentle, easy to be entreated, full of mercy and good fruits, without partiality and without hypocrisy[1]."

In all these passages, one and the same character is described acceptable to God, unacceptable to man; unacceptable to man both in itself, and because it involves a change, and that a painful one, in one shape or other. Nothing short of suffering, except in rare cases, makes

[1] James iii. 17.

us what we should be; gentle instead of harsh, meek instead of violent, conceding instead of arrogant, lowly instead of proud, pure-hearted instead of sensual, sensitive of sin instead of carnal. This is the especial object which is set before us, to become holy as He who has called us is holy, and to discipline and chasten ourselves in order that we may become so; and we may be quite sure, that unless we chasten ourselves, God will chasten us. If we judge ourselves, through His mercy we shall not be judged of Him; if we do not afflict ourselves in light things, He will afflict us in heavy things; if we do not set about changing ourselves by gentle measures, He will change us by severe remedies. "I refrain my soul," says David, "and keep it low, like as a child that is weaned from his mother." "I keep under my body, and bring it into subjection," says St. Paul. Of course Satan will try to turn all our attempts to his own purposes. He will try to make us think too much of ourselves for what we do; he would fain make us despise others; he will try to ensnare us in other ways. Of course he turns all things to evil, as far as he can; all our crosses may become temptations: illness, affliction, bereavement, pain, loss of worldly prospects, anxiety, all may be instruments of evil; so likewise may all methods of self-chastisement, but they ought not to be, and need not. And their legitimate effect, through the grace of the Holy Spirit, is to make us like Him who suffered all pain, physical and moral, sin excepted, in its fulness.

We know what His character was; how grave and subdued His speech, His manner, His acts; what calmness,
self-possession, tenderness, and endurance; how He re-
sisted evil; how He turned His cheek to the smiter;
how He blessed when persecuted; how He resigned
Himself to His God and Father, how He suffered
silently, and opened not His mouth, when accused mali-
ciously.

Alas! so it is; not only does the world not imitate
such a temper of mind as this; but, if the truth must be
spoken, it despises it. As regards, indeed, our Lord's
instance itself, the force of education, habit, custom, fear
of each other, and some remaining awe, keep the world
from reflecting upon the notes of character which the
Gospels ascribe to Him, but in His followers, it does discern them, it understands and it condemns them. We are
bidden lend and give, asking for nothing again; revenge
not ourselves; give our cloak when our coat is taken;
offer the left cheek when the right is smitten; suffer
without complaint; account persons better than they
are; keep from bitter words; pray only when others
would be impatient to act; deny ourselves for the sake
of others; live contented with what we are; preserve an
ignorance of sin and of the world: what is all this, but
a character of mind which the world scorns and ridicules
even more than it hates? a character which seems to
court insult, because it endures it? Is not this what
men of the world would say of such a one? " Such a man

is unfit for life; he has no eye for any thing; he does not know the difference between good and evil; he is tame and spiritless, he is simple and dull, and a fit prey for the spoiler or defrauder; he is cowardly and narrow-minded, unmanly, feeble, superstitious, and a dreamer," with many other words more contemptuous and more familiar than would be becoming to use in Church. Yet such is the character of which Christ gave us the pattern; such was the character of Apostles; such the character which has ever conquered the world. "In much patience, in afflictions, in necessities, in distresses, in stripes, in imprisonments, in watchings, in fastings, by pureness, by knowledge, by long-suffering, by kindness, by the Holy Ghost, by love unfeigned, by the word of truth, by the power of God, by the armour of righteousness on the right hand and on the left, by honour and dishonour, by evil report and good report, as deceivers and yet true, as chastened and not killed, as sorrowful yet alway rejoicing;"—these are the weapons of our warfare, "which are not carnal, but mighty through God to the pulling down of strong holds[1]." These are despised by the world, but they have subdued the world. Nay, though they seem most unmanly, they in the event have proved most heroic. For the heroical character springs out of them. He who has thrown himself out of this world, alone can overcome it; he who has cut himself loose of it, alone cannot be touched by

[1] 2 Cor. vi. 4—10; x. 4.

it; he alone can be courageous, who does not fear it; he alone firm, who is not moved by it; he alone severe with it, who does not love it. Despair makes men bold, and so it is that he who has nothing to hope from the world, has nothing to fear from it. He who has really tasted of the true Cross, can taste no bitterer pain, no keener joy.

I have been trying to urge on you, my brethren, that the taking of Christ's yoke, and learning of Him, is something very distinct and special, and very unlike any other service and character. It is the result of a change from a state of nature, a change so great as to be called a death or even a crucifixion of our natural state. Never allow yourselves, my brethren, to fancy that the true Christian character can coalesce with this world's character, or is the world's character improved— merely a superior kind of worldly character. No, it is a new character; or, as St. Paul words it, "a new creation." Speaking of the Cross of Christ, he says, "God forbid that I should glory, save in the Cross of our Lord Jesus Christ, by whom the world is crucified unto me, and I unto the world. For in Christ Jesus neither circumcision availeth any thing, nor uncircum-cision, but a new creature[1]." It is a new character, and it is one; it is ever one and the same. It is not one in Apostles, and another in the Christian of this day; not one in the high, another in the low; one in

[1] .Gal. vi. 14, 15.

rich, another in poor; one in Englishman, another in foreigner; one in man, another in woman. Where Christ is put on, St. Paul tells us, there is neither Jew nor Greek, bond nor free, male nor female, but all are one in Christ Jesus[1]. What Lazarus is, that must Dives become; what Apostles were, that must each of us be. The high in this world think it suitable in them to show a certain pride and self-confidence; the wealthy claim deference on account of their wealth; kings and princes think themselves above instruction from any; men in the middle ranks consider it enough to be decent and respectable, and deem sanctity superfluous in them; the poor think to be saved by their poverty;—but to one and all Christ speaks, " Come unto Me," " Learn of Me." There is but one Cross and one character of mind formed by it; and nothing can be further from it than those tempers and dispositions in which the greater part of men called Christians live. To have one's own way, to follow one's own tastes, to please one's self, to have things to one's mind, not to be thwarted, to indulge in the comforts of life, to do little for God, to think of Him now and then indeed, but to live to this world; to aim at things of this world; to judge of things by our own accidental judgment, be it better or worse; to measure religious men, to decide upon right or wrong in religion, by our favourite fancy; to take a pride in forming and maintaining our own opinion; to stand

[1] Gal. iii. 28.

upon our rights; to fear the hard words and cold looks of men, to be afraid of being too religious, to dread singularity; to leave our hearts and minds, our thoughts, words, and actions, to take care of themselves :—this, on one side or the other, in this measure or that, is the sort of character which the multitude, even of what are called respectable men, exemplify; and no wonder, this being the case, that they speak against those who have, or strive to have, a more serious view of religion, and whose mode of living condemns them. If there be but one character of heart that can please God, both of these contrary characters cannot please Him, one or the other does not; if the easy religion is right, the strict religion is wrong; if strict religion is right, easy religion is wrong. Let us not deceive ourselves; there are not two ways of salvation—a broad and a narrow. The world, which chooses the broad way, in consequence hates and spurns the narrow way; and in turn our Blessed Lord, who has chosen for us the narrow way, hates, scorns, spurns, denounces, the broad way. Surely He does so; He hates the broad way as entirely as the world hates the narrow way; and if we are persuaded to take part with the world, we take part against Him. When St. Peter said, "Be it far from Thee, Lord," being shocked at the notice that his Lord should suffer, what was His answer? Did He thank him for his zeal? Did He, at least, let it pass in silence? He answered, "Get thee behind Me, Satan, for thou art an

offence unto Me; for thou savourest not the things that
be of God, but those that be of men[1]." And in like
manner to the corrupt church of Laodicea He says,
" Because thou art lukewarm, and neither cold nor hot,
I will cast thee out of My mouth. Because thou sayest,
I am rich, and increased with goods, and have need of
nothing; and knowest not, that thou art wretched and
miserable, and poor, and blind, and naked; I counsel
thee to buy of Me gold tried in the fire, that thou
mayest be rich, and white raiment, that thou mayest
be clothed; and anoint thine eyes with eye-salve, that
thou mayest see." And then He adds: " As many as I
love, I rebuke and chasten;" that is, He puts on them
His yoke; " Be zealous therefore and repent[2]."

To conclude. If Almighty God moves any of us, so
that we have high thoughts; if from reading Scripture
or holy books we find that we can embrace views above
the world; if it is given us to recognize the glory of
Christ's kingdom, to discern its spiritual nature, to
admire the life of saints, and to desire to imitate it; if
we feel and understand that it is good to bear the yoke
in our youth, good to be in trouble, good to be poor,
good to be in low estate, good to be despised; if in
imagination we put ourselves at the feet of those mortified men of old time, who, after St. Paul's pattern, died
daily, and knew no one after the flesh; if we feel all
this, and are conscious we feel it; let us not boast—why?

[1] Matt. xvi. 23.   [2] Rev. iii. 16—19.

because of a surety such feelings are a pledge to us that God will in some way or other give them exercise. He gives them to us that He may use them. He gives us the opportunity of using them. Dare not to indulge in high thoughts; be cautious of them, and refrain; they are the shadows of coming trials; they are not given for nothing; they are given for an end; that end is coming. My brethren, count the cost; never does God give faith but He tries it; never does He implant the wish to sit on His right hand and on His left, but He fulfils it by making us wash our brethren's feet. O fearful imaginations, which are sure to be realized! O dangerous wishes, which are heard and forthwith answered! Only may God temper things to us, that nothing may be beyond our strength!

SERMON IX.

MOSES THE TYPE OF CHRIST.

DEUT. xviii. 15.

" The Lord thy God will raise up unto thee a Prophet from the midst of thee, of thy brethren, like unto me; unto Him ye shall hearken."

THE history of Moses is valuable to Christians, not only as giving us a pattern of fidelity towards God, of great firmness, and great meekness, but also as affording us a type or figure of our Saviour Christ. No prophet arose in Israel like Moses, till Christ came, when the promise in the text was fulfilled—" The Lord thy God," says Moses, " shall raise up unto thee a Prophet like unto me :" that was Christ. Now let us consider in what respects Moses resembled Christ; we shall find that this inquiry is very suitable at this time of year [1].

1. First, if we survey the general history of the Israelites, we shall find that it is a picture of man's history, as the dispensation of the Gospel displays it to us, and that in it Moses takes the place of Christ. The

[1] Lent.

Israelites were in the land of strangers, viz. the Egyptians; they were slaves, hardly tasked, and wretched, and God broke their bonds, led them out of Egypt, after many perils, to the promised land, Canaan, a land flowing with milk and honey. How clearly this prefigures to us the condition of the Christian Church! We are by nature in a strange country; God was our first Father, and His Presence our dwelling-place: but we were cast out of paradise for sinning, and are in a dreary land, a valley of darkness and the shadow of death. We are born in this spiritual Egypt, the land of strangers. Still we have old recollections about us, and broken traditions, of our original happiness and dignity as freemen. Thoughts come across us from time to time which show that we were born for better things than to be slaves; yet by nature slaves we are, slaves to the Devil. He is our hard task-master, as Pharaoh oppressed the Israelites; so much the worse than he, in that his chains, though we do not see them, become more and more heavy every year. They cling about us and grow; they multiply themselves, they shoot out and spread forth, and encircle us, those chains of sin, with many links, minute but heavy, weighing us down to the earth, till at last we are mere slaves of the soil, with an evil husbandry, slaves of that fearful harvest which is eternal death. Satan is a tyrant over us, and it seems to us useless to rebel. If we attempt it, we are but overpowered by his huge might, and his oppressive rule, and are made twice the children of hell that we were before : we may groan and look about, but we cannot fly from his country. Such is our state by nature.

But Moses conducted the Israelites from the house of bondage to their own land, from which their fathers had descended into Egypt. He came to them from God, and, armed with God's power, he smote their cruel enemies, led them out of Pharaoh's territory, divided the Red Sea, carried them through it, and at length brought them to the borders of Canaan. And who is it that has done this for us Christians? Who but the Eternal Son of God, our Lord and Saviour, whose name in consequence we bear? He has rescued us from the arm of him who was stronger than we; and therefore I say in this respect first of all, Christ is a second Moses, and a greater. Christ has broken the power of the Devil. He leads us forth on our way, and makes a path through all difficulties, that we may go forward towards heaven. Most men, who have deliberately turned their hearts to seek God, must recollect times when the view of the difficulties which lay before them, and of their own weakness, nearly made them sink through fear. Then they were like the children of Israel on the shore of the Red Sea. How boisterous did the waves look! and they could not see beyond them; they seemed taken by their enemies as in a net. Pharaoh with his horsemen hurried on to reclaim his runaway slaves; the Israelites sank down in terror on the sand of the sea-shore; every moment brought death or captivity nearer to them. Then it was that Moses said, "Stand still, and see the salvation of God." And in like manner has Christ spoken to us. When our hearts fainted within us, when we said to ourselves, "How is it possible that we should attain heaven?" When we felt how desirable it was to serve God, but felt keenly the power of temptation; when we acknowledged in our hearts that God was holy and most adorable, and obedience to His will most lovely and admirable, and yet recollected instances of our past disobedience, and feared lest all our renewed resolutions to serve Him would be broken and swept away by the old Adam as mercilessly as heretofore, and that Satan would regain us, and yet prayed earnestly to God for His saving help; then He saved us against our fear, surprising us by the strangeness of our salvation. This, I say, many a one must recollect in his own case. It happens to Christians not once, but again and again through life. Troubles are lightened, trials are surmounted, fears disappear. We are enabled to do things above our strength by trusting to Christ; we overcome our most urgent sins, we surrender our most innocent wishes; we conquer ourselves; we make a way through the powers of the world, the flesh, and the devil; the waves divide, and our Lord, the great Captain of our salvation, leads us over. Christ, then, is a second Moses, and greater than he, inasmuch as Christ leads from hell to heaven, as Moses led the Israelites from Egypt to Canaan.

2. Next, Christ reveals to us the will of God, as Moses to the Israelites. He is our Prophet, as well as our Redeemer. None was so favoured as Moses in this respect: before Christ came, Moses alone saw God face to face; all prophets after him but heard His voice or saw Him in vision. Samuel was called by name, but he knew not who called him in the dark night till Eli told him. Isaiah saw the vision of the Seraphim, and heard them cry "Holy" before the Lord; but it was not heaven that he saw, but the mere semblance of the earthly temple in which God dwelt among the Jews, and clouds filled it. But Moses in some sense saw God and lived; thus God honoured him. "If there be a prophet among you," said Almighty God, "I the Lord will make Myself known unto him in a vision, and will speak unto him in a dream. My servant Moses is not so, who is faithful in all Mine house. With him will I speak mouth to mouth, even apparently, and not in dark speeches, and the similitude of the Lord shall he behold [1]:" and on his death we are told, "there arose not a prophet since in Israel like unto Moses, whom the Lord knew face to face [2]." When he was in the Mount Sinai it is said of him still more expressly, "The Lord spake unto Moses face to face, as a man speaketh unto his friend [3]." In the Mount he received from God the

[1] Numb. xii. 6—8.   [2] Deut. xxxiv. 10.   [3] Exod. xxxiii. 11.

revelation of the Law, and the patterns of the holy services which the Jews were to offer to God; and so, being favoured with the intimate knowledge of God's counsels, when he came down, his face shone with glory. The Divine majesty was reflected from it, and the people dared not look upon him. "The skin of his face shone while he talked with Him. And when Aaron and the children of Israel saw Moses, they were afraid to come nigh him." "And till he had done speaking with them, he put a veil on his face [1]."

Yet, after all, favoured as he was, Moses saw not the true presence of God. Flesh and blood cannot see it. Even when Moses was in the Mount, he was aware that the very fulness of God's glory then revealed to him, was after all but the surface of His infinitude. The more he saw, the deeper and wider did he know that to be which he saw not. He prayed, "If I have found grace in Thy sight, show me now Thy way, that I may know Thee, that I may find grace in Thy sight; and God said, My Presence shall go with thee, and I will give thee rest [2]." Moses was encouraged to ask for further blessings; he said, "I beseech Thee, show me Thy glory." This could not be granted; "Thou canst not see My face; for there shall no man see Me, and live." So, as the greatest privilege which he might attain, Moses was permitted to see the skirts of God's greatness—"The Lord passed by in a cloud, and pro-

[1] Exod. xxxiv. 29, 30. 33. [2] Exod. xxxiii. 13, 14.

claimed the Name of the Lord; and Moses made haste, and bowed his head toward the earth, and worshipped [1]." And it was this sight of the mere apparel in which God Almighty was arrayed, which made his face to shine.

But Christ really saw, and ever saw, the face of God, for He was no creature of God, but the Only-begotten Son, who is in the bosom of the Father. From eternity He was with Him in glory, as He says Himself, dwelling in the abyss of the infinite greatness of the Most High. Not for forty days, as Moses on the mount in figure, but for ever and ever was He present as the Counsellor of God, as His Word, in whom He delighted. Such was He of old; but at the time appointed He came forth from the Father, and showed Himself in this external world, first as its Creator, then as its Teacher, the Revealer of secrets, the Mediator, the Off-streaming of God's glory, and the Express Image of His Person. Cloud nor image, emblem nor words, are interposed between the Son and His Eternal Father. No language is needed between the Father and Him, who is the very Word of the Father; no knowledge is imparted to Him, who by His very Nature and from eternity knows the Father, and all that the Father knows. Such are His own words, " No man knoweth the Son but the Father, neither knoweth any man the Father save the Son, and he to whomsoever the Son will reveal Him [2]." Again He says, " He that hath seen Me hath

[1] Exod. xxxiv. 6. 8.   [2] Matt. xi. 27.

seen the Father[1];" and He accounts for this when He tells us, that He and the Father are one[2]; and that He is in the bosom of the Father, and so can disclose Him to mankind, being still in heaven, even while He was on earth.

Accordingly, the Blessed Apostle draws a contrast between Moses and Christ to our comfort; "the Law," he says, "was given by Moses, but grace and truth came by Jesus Christ[3]." In Him·God is fully and truly seen, so that He is absolutely the Way, and the Truth, and the Life. All our duties are summed up for us in the message He brings us. Those who look towards Him for teaching, who worship and obey Him, will by degrees see "the light of the knowledge of the glory of God in His face," and will be "changed into the same image from glory to glory." And thus it happens that men of the lowest class and the humblest education may know fully the ways and works of God; fully, that is, as man can know them; far better and more truly than the most sagacious man of this world, to whom the Gospel is hid. Religion has a store of wonderful secrets which no one can communicate to another, and which are most pleasant and delightful to know. "Call on Me," says God by the prophet, "and I will answer thee, and show thee great and mighty things which thou knowest not of." This is no mere idle boast, but a fact which all who seek God

---

[1] John xiv. 9.   [2] John x. 30.   [3] John i. 17.

will find to be true, though they cannot perhaps clearly express their meaning. Strange truths about ourselves, about God, about our duty, about the world, about heaven and hell, new modes of viewing things, discoveries which cannot be put into words, marvellous prospects and thoughts half understood, deep convictions inspiring joy and peace, these are a part of the revelation which Christ, the Son of God, brings to those who obey Him. Moses had much toil to gain from the great God some scattered rays of the truth, and that for his personal comfort, not for all Israel; but Christ has brought from His Father for all of us the full and perfect way of life. Thus He brings grace as well as truth, a most surprising miracle of mercy from the freeness of the gift, as well as a true wisdom from its fulness.

And yet, alas! in spite of all this bounty, men called Christians, and how many! live heartlessly, not caring for the gracious benefit. Look at the world. Men begin life with sinning; they quench the early promise of grace, and defile their souls; they block up the entrances of the spiritual senses by acts of sin, lying and deceit, intemperance, profaneness, or uncleanness,—by a foolish and trifling turn of mind,—by neglect of prayer when there is no actual vice,—or by an obstinate selfishness. How many are the ways in which men begin to lose sight of God!—how many are the fallings away of those who once began well! And then they soon forget that they have really left God; they still think they see His face, though their sins have begun to blind them. Like men who fall asleep, the real prospect still flits before them in their dreams, but out of shape and proportion, discoloured, crowded with all manner of fancies and untruths; and so they proceed in that dream of sin, more or less profound,—sometimes rousing, then turning back again for a little more slumber, till death awakens them. Death alone gives lively perceptions to the generality of men, who then see the very truth, such as they saw it before they began to sin, but more clear and more fearful: but they who are the pure in heart, like Joseph; or the meek among men, like Moses; or faithful found among the faithless, as Daniel; these men see God all through life in the face of His Eternal Son; and, while the world mocks them, or tries to reason them out of their own real knowledge, they are like Moses on the mount, blessed and hidden,— "hid with Christ in God," beyond the tumult and idols of the world, and interceding for it.

3. This leads me to mention a third point of resemblance between Moses and Christ. Moses was the great intercessor when the Israelites sinned: while he was in the mount, his people corrupted themselves; they set up an idol, and honoured it with feasting and dancing. Then God would have cut them off from the land of promise, had not Moses interposed. He said, "Lord, why doth Thy wrath wax hot against Thy

people? Turn from Thy fierce wrath, and repent of this evil against Thy people[1]." In this way he gained a respite, and then he renewed his supplications. He said to the people, " Ye have sinned a great sin ; but now I will go up unto the Lord : peradventure I shall make an atonement for your sin." Then he said to their offended Creator, " Oh, this people have sinned a great sin, and have made them gods of gold. Yet now, if Thou wilt, forgive their sin."

Here Moses, as is obvious, shadows out the true Mediator between God and man, who is ever at the right hand of God making intercession for us ; but the parallel is closer still than appears at first sight. After Moses had said, " If Thou wilt, forgive their sin," he added, " and if not, blot me, I pray Thee, out of Thy book, which Thou hast written." He was taken at his word. Observe, rather than Israel should forfeit the promised land, he here offered to give up his own portion in it, and the exchange was accepted. He was excluded, dying in sight, not in enjoyment of Canaan, while the people went in under Joshua. This was a figure of Him that was to come. Our Saviour Christ died, that we might live : He consented to lose the light of God's countenance, that we might gain it. By His cross and passion, He made atonement for our sins, and bought for us the forgiveness of God. Yet, on the other hand, observe how this history instructs us, at the

[1] Exod. xxxii. 11.

same time, in the unspeakable distance between Christ and Moses. When Moses said, "Blot me, I pray Thee, out of Thy book," God did not promise to accept the exchange, but He answered, "Whosover hath sinned against Me, him will I blot out of My book." Moses was not taken instead of Israel, except in figure. In spite of Moses, the sinful people were plagued and died[1], though their children entered the promised land. And again, Moses, after all, suffered for his own sin. True, he was shut out from Canaan. But why? Not in spite of his having "done nothing amiss," as the Divine Sufferer on the cross, but because he spake unadvisedly with his lips, when the people provoked him with their murmurings. The meek Moses was provoked to call them rebels, and seemed to arrogate to himself the power and authority which he received from God; and therefore he was punished by dying in the wilderness. But Christ was the spotless Lamb of God, "who, when He was reviled, reviled not again; when He suffered, He threatened not, but committed Himself to Him that judgeth righteously." And His death is meritorious; it has really gained our pardon.

Moreover, it is well to observe how apparently slight a fault it was for which Moses suffered; for this shows us the infinite difference between the best of a sinful race and Him who was sinless,—the least taint of human corruption having in it an unspeakable evil.

[1] Vide Exod. xxxii. 34.

Moses was the meekest of men, yet it was for one
sudden transgression of the rule of meekness that he
suffered; all his former gentleness, all his habitual
humbleness of mind, availed him nothing. It was
unprofitable, and without merit, because it was merely
his duty. It could not make up for a single sin,
however slight. Thus we see how it would be with us
if God were extreme to mark what is done amiss: and
thus, on the other hand, we see how supremely holy and
pure that Saviour must be whose intercession is meritorious, who has removed from us God's anger. None
can bring us to Him but He who came from Him. He
reveals God, and He cleanses man. The same is our
Prophet and our Priest.

We are now approaching the season when we commemorate His death upon the cross: we are entering
upon the most holy season of the whole year. May we
approach it with holy hearts! May we renew our
resolutions of leading a life of obedience to His commandments, and may we have the grace to seal our good
resolutions at His most sacred Supper, in which " Jesus
Christ is evidently set forth crucified among us." It
is useless to make resolves without coming to Him for
aid to keep them; and it is useless coming to His table
without earnest and hearty resolves; it is provoking
God " to plague us with divers diseases, and sundry
kinds of death." But what shall be said of those who
do neither the one nor the other,—who neither vow

obedience, nor come to Him for grace?—who sin deliberately after they have known the truth—who review their sins in time past in a reckless hard-hearted way, or put them aside out of their thoughts—who can bear to jest about them, to speak of them to others unblushingly, or even to boast of them, and to determine on sinning again,—who think of repenting at some future day, and resolve on going their own way now, trusting to chance for reconciliation with God, as if it were not a matter to be very anxious about? This state of mind brings upon man a judgment heavier than all the plagues of Egypt,—a judgment compared with which that darkness which could be felt is as the sun's brightness, and the thunders and hail are as the serene sky,—the wrath to come.

Awake, then, my brethren, with this season, to meet your God, who now summons you from His cross and tomb. Put aside the sin that doth so easily beset you, and be ye holy even as He is holy. Stand ready to suffer with Him, should it be needful, that you may rise together with Him. He can make bitter things sweet to you, and hard ways easy, if you have but the heart to desire Him to do so. He can change the Law into the Gospel. He can, for Moses, give you Himself. He can write the Law on your hearts, and thereby take away the hand-writing that is against you, even the old curse which by nature you inherit. He has done this for many in time past. He does it for many at all times.

Why should He not do it for you? Why should you be left out? Why should you not enter into His rest? Why should you not see His glory? O, why should you be blotted out from His book?

SERMON X.

THE CRUCIFIXION.

ISAIAH liii. 7.

" He was oppressed, and He was afflicted, yet He opened not His mouth; He is brought as a lamb to the slaughter, and as a sheep before her shearers is dumb, so He openeth not His mouth."

ST. PETER makes it almost a description of a Christian, that he loves Him whom he has not seen; speaking of Christ, he says, "whom having not seen, ye love; in whom, though now ye see Him not, yet believing, ye rejoice with joy unspeakable and full of glory." Again he speaks of "tasting that the Lord is gracious[1]." Unless we have a true love of Christ, we are not His true disciples; and we cannot love Him unless we have heartfelt gratitude to Him; and we cannot duly feel gratitude, unless we feel keenly what He suffered for us. I say it seems to us impossible, under the circumstances of the case, that any one can have attained to the love of Christ, who feels no distress, no misery, at the thought of His bitter pains, and no self-reproach at

[1] 1 Pet. i. 8; ii. 3.

having through his own sins had a share in causing them.

I know quite well, and wish you, my brethren, never to forget, that feeling is not enough; that it is not enough merely to feel and nothing more; that to feel grief for Christ's sufferings, and yet not to go on to obey Him, is not true love, but a mockery. True love both feels right, and acts right; but at the same time as warm feelings without religious conduct are a kind of hypocrisy, so, on the other hand, right conduct, when unattended with deep feelings, is at best a very imperfect sort of religion. And at this time of year[1] especially are we called upon to raise our hearts to Christ, and to have keen feelings and piercing thoughts of sorrow and shame, of compunction and of gratitude, of love and tender affection and horror and anguish, at the review of those awful sufferings whereby our salvation has been purchased.

Let us pray God to give us *all* graces; and while, in the first place, we pray that He would make us holy, really holy, let us also pray Him to give us the *beauty* of holiness, which consists in tender and eager affection towards our Lord and Saviour; which is, in the case of the Christian, what beauty of person is to the outward man, so that through God's mercy our souls may have, not strength and health only, but a sort of bloom and comeliness; and that as we grow older in body, we may, year by year, grow more youthful in spirit.

[1] Passion-tide.

You will ask, *how* are we to learn to feel pain and anguish at the thought of Christ's sufferings? I answer, *by* thinking of them, that is, by *dwelling* on the thought. This, through God's mercy, is in the power of every one. No one who will but solemnly think over the history of those sufferings, as drawn out for us in the Gospels, but will gradually gain, through God's grace, a sense of them, will in a measure realize them, will in a measure be as if he saw them, will feel towards them as being not merely a tale written in a book, but as a true history, as a series of events which took place. It is indeed a great mercy that this duty which I speak of, though so high, is notwithstanding so level with the powers of all classes of persons, learned and unlearned, if they wish to perform it. Any one can think of Christ's sufferings, if he will; and knows well what to think about. "It is not in heaven that thou shouldst say, Who shall go up for us to heaven and bring it to us, that we may hear it and do it? Neither is it beyond the sea that thou shouldst say, Who shall go over the sea for us? . . . but the word is very nigh unto thee;" very nigh, for it is in the four Gospels, which, at this day at least, are open to all men. All men may read or hear the Gospels, and in knowing them, they will know all that is necessary to be known in order to feel aright; they will know all that any one knows, all that has been told us, all that the greatest saints have ever had to make them full of love and sacred fear.

Now, then, let me make one or two reflections by way of stirring up your hearts and making you mourn over Christ's sufferings, as you are called to do at this season.

I. First, as to these sufferings you will observe that our Lord is called a lamb, in the text; that is, He was as defenceless, and as innocent, as a lamb is. Since then Scripture compares Him to this inoffensive and unprotected animal, we may without presumption or irreverence take the image as a means of conveying to our minds those feelings which our Lord's sufferings should excite in us. I mean, consider how very horrible it is to read the accounts which sometimes meet us of cruelties exercised on brute animals. Does it not sometimes make us shudder to hear tell of them, or to read them in some chance publication which we take up? At one time it is the wanton deed of barbarous and angry owners who ill-treat their cattle, or beasts of burden; and at another, it is the cold-blooded and calculating act of men of science, who make experiments on brute animals, perhaps merely from a sort of curiosity. I do not like to go into particulars, for many reasons; but one of those instances which we read of as happening in this day, and which seems more shocking than the rest, is, when the poor dumb victim is fastened against a wall, pierced, gashed, and so left to linger out its life. Now do you not see that I have a reason for saying this, and am not using these distressing words for nothing? For what was this but the very cruelty inflicted upon our

Lord? He was gashed with the scourge, pierced through hands and feet, and so fastened to the Cross, and there left, and that as a spectacle. Now what is it moves our very hearts, and sickens us so much at cruelty shown to poor brutes? I suppose this first, that they have done no harm; next, that they have no power whatever of resistance; it is the cowardice and tyranny of which they are the victims which makes their sufferings so especially touching. For instance, if they were dangerous animals, take the case of wild beasts at large, able not only to defend themselves, but even to attack us; much as we might dislike to hear of their wounds and agony, yet our feelings would be of a very different kind; but there is something so very dreadful, so satanic in tormenting those who never have harmed us, and who cannot defend themselves, who are utterly in our power, who have weapons neither of offence nor defence, that none but very hardened persons can endure the thought of it. Now this was just our Saviour's case: He had laid aside His glory, He had (as it were) disbanded His legions of Angels, He came on earth without arms, except the arms of truth, meekness, and righteousness, and committed Himself to the world in perfect innocence and sinlessness, and in utter helplessness, as the Lamb of God. In the words of St. Peter, "Who did no sin, neither was guile found in His mouth; who, when He was reviled, reviled not again; when He suffered, He threatened not; but committed Himself to Him that judgeth righteously[1]." Think then, my brethren, of your feelings at cruelty practised upon brute animals, and you will gain one sort of feeling which the history of Christ's Cross and Passion ought to excite within you. And let me add, this is in all cases one good use to which you may turn any accounts you read of wanton and unfeeling acts shown towards the inferior animals; let them remind you, as a picture, of Christ's sufferings. He who is higher than the Angels, deigned to humble Himself even to the state of the brute creation, as the Psalm says, "I am a worm, and no man; a very scorn of men, and the outcast of the people[2]."

2. Take another example, and you will see the same thing still more strikingly. How overpowered should we be, nay not at the sight only, but at the very hearing of cruelties shown to a little child, and why so? for the same two reasons, because it was so innocent, and because it was so unable to defend itself. I do not like to go into the details of such cruelty, they would be so heart-rending. What if wicked men took and crucified a young child? What if they deliberately seized its poor little frame, and stretched out its arms, nailed them to a cross bar of wood, drove a stake through its two feet, and fastened them to a beam, and so left it to die? It is almost too shocking to say perhaps, you will actually say it *is* too shocking, and ought not to be said. O, my brethren, you feel the horror of this, and

yet you can bear to read of Christ's sufferings without horror; for what is that little child's agony to His? and which deserved it more? which is the more innocent? which the holier? was He not gentler, sweeter, meeker, more tender, more loving, than any little child? Why are you shocked at the one, why are you not shocked at the other?

Or take another instance, not so shocking in its circumstances, yet introducing us to another distinction, in which Christ's passion exceeds that of any innocent sufferers, such as I have supposed. When Joseph was sent by his father to his brethren on a message of love, they, when they saw him, said, "Behold, this dreamer cometh; come now, therefore, and let us slay him[1]." They did not kill him, however, but they put him in a pit in spite of the anguish of his soul, and sold him as a slave to the Ishmaelites, and he was taken down into a foreign country, where he had no friends. Now this was most cruel and most cowardly in the sons of Jacob; and what is so especially shocking in it is, that Joseph was not only innocent and defenceless, their younger brother whom they ought to have protected, but besides that, he was so confiding and loving, that he need not have come to them, that he would not at all have been in their power, *except* for his desire to do them service. Now, whom does this history remind us of but of Him concerning whom the Master of the vineyard said, on

[1] Gen. xxxvii. 19, 20.

sending Him to the husbandmen, "They will reverence
My Son¹?" "But when the husbandmen saw the Son,
they said among themselves, This is the Heir, come, let
us kill Him, and let us seize on His inheritance. And
they caught Him, and cast Him out of the vineyard,
and slew Him." Here, then, is an additional circumstance of cruelty to affect us in Christ's history, such
as is suggested in Joseph's, but which no instance of a
brute animal's or of a child's sufferings can have; our
Lord was not only guiltless and defenceless, but He had
come among His persecutors in love.

3. And now, instead of taking the case of the young,
innocent, and confiding, let us take another instance
which will present to us our Lord's passion under
another aspect. Let us suppose that some aged and
venerable person whom we have known as long as we
could recollect any thing, and loved and reverenced,
suppose such a one, who had often done us kindnesses,
who had taught us, who had given us good advice,
who had encouraged us, smiled on us, comforted us in
trouble, whom we knew to be very good and religious,
very holy, full of wisdom, full of heaven, with grey
hairs and awful countenance, waiting for Almighty
God's summons to leave this world for a better place;
suppose, I say, such a one whom we have ourselves
known, and whose memory is dear to us, rudely seized
by fierce men, stripped naked in public, insulted, driven

¹ Matt. xxi. 37—39.

about here and there, made a laughing-stock, struck, spit on, dressed up in other clothes in ridicule, then severely scourged on the back, then laden with some heavy load till he could carry it no longer, pulled and dragged about, and at last exposed with all his wounds to the gaze of a rude multitude who came and jeered him, what would be our feelings? Let us in our mind think of this person or that, and consider how we should be overwhelmed and pierced through and through by such a hideous occurrence.

But what is all this to the suffering of the holy Jesus, which we bear to read of as a matter of course! [Only think of Him, when in His wounded state, and without garment on, He had to creep up the ladder, as He could, which led Him up the cross high enough for His murderers to nail Him to it; and consider *who* it was that was in that misery.] Or again, view Him dying, hour after hour bleeding to death; and how? in peace? no; with His arms stretched out, and His face exposed to view, and any one who pleased coming and staring at Him, mocking Him, and watching the gradual ebbing of His strength, and the approach of death. These are some of the appalling details which the Gospels contain, and surely they were not recorded for nothing; but that we might dwell on them.

Do you think that those who saw these things had much heart for eating or drinking or enjoying themselves? On the contrary, we are told that even "the people who came together to that sight, smote their breasts and returned[1]." If these were the feelings of the people, what were St. John's feelings, or St. Mary Magdalene's, or St. Mary's, our Lord's blessed mother? Do we desire to be of this company? do we desire, according to His own promise, to be rather blessed than the womb that bare Him, and the paps that He sucked? do we desire to be as His brother, and sister, and mother[2]? Then, surely, ought we to have some portion of that mother's sorrow! When He was on the cross and she stood by, then, according to Simeon's prophecy, "a sword pierced through her soul[3]." What is the use of our keeping the memory of His cross and passion, unless we lament and are in sorrow with her? I can understand people who do not keep Good Friday at all; they are indeed very ungrateful, but I know what they mean; I understand them. But I do not understand at all, I do not at all see what men mean who *do* profess to keep it, yet do not sorrow, or at least try to sorrow. Such a spirit of grief and lamentation is expressly mentioned in Scripture as a characteristic of those who turn to Christ. If then *we* do not sorrow, have *we* turned to Him? "I will pour upon the house of David," says the merciful Saviour Himself, before He came on earth, speaking of what was to come, "upon the inhabitants of Jerusalem, the spirit of grace and of supplications; and they shall look upon Me

[1] Luke xxiii. 48.　　[2] Matt. xii. 46, &c.　　[3] Luke ii. 35.

whom they have pierced, and they shall *mourn* for Him, as one mourneth for his only son, and shall be in bitterness for Him, as one that is in bitterness for his firstborn [1]."

One thing I will add :—if there be persons here present who are conscious to themselves that they do not feel the grief which this season should cause them, who feel now as they do at other times, let them consider with themselves whether perhaps this defect does not arise from their having neglected to come to church, whether during this season or at other times, as often as they might. Our feelings are not in our own power; God alone can rule our feelings; God alone can make us sorrow, when we would but cannot sorrow; but *will* He, if we have not diligently sought Him according to our opportunities in this house of grace? I speak of those who might come to prayers more frequently, and do not. I know well that many cannot come. I speak of those who can, if they will. Even if they come as often as they are able, I know well they will not be *satisfied* with their own feelings; they will be conscious even then that they ought to grieve more than they do of course none of us feels the great event of this day as he ought, and therefore we all *ought* to be dissatisfied with ourselves. However, if this is not our own fault, we need not be out of heart, for God will mercifully lead us forward in His own time; but if it arises from our

[1] Zech. xii. 10.

not coming to prayers here as often as we might, then our coldness and deadness *are* our own fault, and I beg you all to consider that that fault is not a slight one. It is said in the Book of Revelation, "Behold He cometh with clouds; and every eye shall see Him, and they also which pierced Him: and all kindreds of the earth shall wail because of Him[1]." We, my brethren, every one of us, shall one day rise from our graves, and see Jesus Christ; we shall see Him who hung on the cross, we shall see His wounds, we shall see the marks in His hands, and in His feet, and in His side. Do we wish to be of those, then, who wail and lament, or of those who rejoice? If we would not lament at the sight of Him then, we must lament at the thought of Him now. Let us prepare to meet our God; let us come into His Presence whenever we can; let us try to fancy as if we saw the Cross and Him upon it; let us draw near to it; let us beg Him to look on us as He did on the penitent thief, and let us say to Him, " Lord remember me when Thou comest in Thy kingdom[2]."

Let this be added to the prayer, my brethren, with which you are about to leave this church. [After I have given the blessing, you will say to yourselves a short prayer.] Well; fancy you see Jesus Christ on the cross, and say to Him with the penitent thief, " Lord, remember me when Thou comest in Thy kingdom;" that is, " Remember me, Lord, in mercy, remember not my sins,

[1] Rev. i. 7.   [2] Luke xxiii. 42.

but Thine own cross; remember Thine own sufferings, remember that Thou sufferedst for me, a sinner; remember in the last day that I, during my lifetime, felt Thy sufferings, that I suffered on my cross by Thy side. Remember me then, and make me remember Thee now."

SERMON XI.

ATTENDANCE ON HOLY COMMUNION.

John v. 40.

"Ye will not come to Me, that ye might have life."

ST. JOHN tells us in to-day's Epistle[1] that "God hath given unto us eternal life, and this life is in His Son. He that hath the Son hath life, and he that hath not the Son hath not life." Yet in the text the Son Himself, our Saviour, sorrowfully and solemnly expostulates with His own brethren, "Ye will not come to Me, that ye might have life." "He came unto His own, and His own received Him not." We know from history, as a matter of fact, that they did not receive Him, that they did not come to Him when He came to them; but He says in the text that they would not come, that they did not wish to come, implying that they, and none else but they, were the cause of their not coming.

Does it not seem a plain natural instinct that every one should seek his own good? What then is meant by

---
[1] First Sunday after Easter.

this unwillingness to come for the greatest of goods, life; an unwillingness, which, guided by the light of Scripture and by experience, we can confidently affirm to prevail at this day as widely and as fully as in the age in which Christ said it?

Here is no question of a comparison of good with good. We cannot account for this unconcern about Christ's gift, by alleging that we have a sufficient treasure in our hands already, and therefore are not interested by the news of a greater. Far from it; for is not the world continually taking away its own gifts, whatever they are? and does it not thereby bring home to us, does it not importunately press upon us, and weary us with the lesson of its own nothingness? Do we not confess that eternal life is the best of all conceivable gifts, before which none other deserve to be mentioned? yet we live to the world.

Nay, and sin also warns us not to trust to its allurements; like the old prophet of Bethel, sin is forced to bear witness against itself, and in the name of the Lord to denounce the Lord's judgments upon us. While it seduces us, it stings us with remorse; and even when the sense of guilt is overcome, still the misery of sinning is inflicted on us in the inward disappointments and the temporal punishments which commonly follow upon transgression. Yet we will not come unto Christ that we may have life.

Further, it is not that God treats us as servants or

slaves; He does not put a burden on us above our strength: He does not repel us from His Presence till we have prepared some offering to bring before Him, or have made some good progress in the way of life. No; He has begun His dealings with us with special, spontaneous acts of mercy. He has, by an inconceivable goodness, sent His Son to be our life. Far from asking any gift at our hands in the first instance, He has from our infancy taken us in charge, and freely given us " all things that pertain unto life and godliness." He has been urgent with us in the very morning of our days, and by the fulness of His grace has anticipated the first stirrings of pride and lust, while as yet sin slept within us. Is it not so? What more could have been done for us? Yet, in spite of all this, men will not come unto Him that they may have life.

So strange is this, that thoughtful persons are some-times tempted to suppose that the mass of mankind do not sufficiently know what their duty is; that they need teaching, else they would be obedient. And others fancy that if the doctrines of the Gospel were set before them in a forcible or persuasive manner, this would serve as a means of rousing them to an habitual sense of their true state. But ignorance is not the true cause why men will not come to Christ.

Who are these willing outcasts from Christ's favour, of whom I speak? Do not think I say a strong thing, my brethren, when I tell you that I am speaking of some of those who now hear me. Not that I dare draw the line any where, or imagine that I can give any rule for knowing for certain, just who come to Him in heart and spirit, and who do not; but I am quite sure that many, who would shrink from giving up their interest in the Gospel, and who profess to cast their lot with Christ, and to trust in His death for their salvation, nevertheless do not really seek Him that they may have life, in spite of their fair speeches. This I say I am too well enabled to know, because in fact so it is, that He has shown us *how* to come to Him, and I see that men do *not* come to Him in that way which He has pointed out. He has shown us, that to come to Him for life is a literal bodily action; not a mere figure, not a mere movement of the heart towards Him, but an action of the visible limbs; not a mere secret faith, but a coming to church, a passing on along the aisle to His holy table, a kneeling down there before Him, and a receiving of the gift of eternal life in the form of bread and wine. There can be no mistaking His own appointment. He said indeed, "He that cometh to Me shall never hunger;" but then He explained what this coming was, by adding, "He that eateth Me, even he shall live by Me." If then a man does not seek Him where He is, there is no profit in seeking Him where He is not. What is the good of sitting at home seeking Him, when His Presence is in the holy Eucharist? Such perverseness is like the sin of the Israelites who went to seek for the manna at a time when it was not given. May not He who gives the gift, prescribe the place and mode of giving it?

Observe how plain and cogent is the proof of what I have been saying. Our Lord declares, " Except ye eat the flesh of the Son of Man, and drink His blood, ye have no life in you:" no life, life being the gift He offers in the text; also He says of the bread which He had broken, " *This* is My Body;" and of the cup, " *This* is My Blood;" is it not very plain, then, that if we refuse to eat that Bread, and drink that Cup, we are refusing to come unto Him that we may have life?

The true reason why people will not come to this Holy Communion is this,—they do not wish to lead religious lives; they do not like to promise to lead religious lives; and they think that that blessed Sacrament does bind them to do so, bind them to live very much more strictly and thoughtfully than they do at present. Allow as much as we will for proper distrust of themselves, reasonable awe, the burden of past sin, imperfect knowledge, and other causes, still after all there is in most cases a reluctance to bear, or at least to pledge themselves to bear, Christ's yoke; a reluctance to give up the service of sin once for all; a lingering love of their own ease, of their own will, of indolence, of carnal habits, of the good opinion of men whom they do not respect; a distrust of their perseverance in holy resolves, grounded on a misgiving about their present sincerity.

This is why men will not come to Christ for life; they know that He will not impart Himself to them, unless they consent to devote themselves to Him.

In what way does He offer Himself to them in Holy Communion? through the commands and sanctions of the Law. First, we are warned against secret sin, and called to self-examination; a week's preparation follows; then, when the time of celebration is come, we hear the Commandments read, we are solemnly exhorted to put off every thing which may offend God; we confess our sins and our deep sorrow for them; lastly, after being admitted to the Sacrament, we expressly bind ourselves to the service of our Lord and Saviour. Doubtless *this* it is which the unrenewed heart cannot bear, the very notion of giving up sin altogether and once for all. And thus, though a gracious voice cry ever so distinctly from the altar, "Come unto Me, and I will refresh you;" and though it be ever so true that this refreshment is nothing short of life, eternal life, yet we recollect the words which follow, "Take My yoke upon you, and learn of Me," and we forthwith murmur and complain, as if the gift were most ungracious, laden with conditions, and hardly purchased, merely because it is offered in that way in which alone a righteous Lord could offer it,—the way of righteousness.

Men had rather give up the promise than implicate themselves in the threats which surround it. Bright and attractive as is the treasure presented to us in the

Gospel, still the pearl of great price lies in its native depths, at the bottom of the ocean. We see it indeed, and know its worth; but not many dare plunge in to bring it thence. What reward offered to the diver shall overcome the imminent peril of a frightful death? and those who love sin, and whose very life consists in habits and practices short of religious, what promised prize can reconcile them to the certain destruction of what they delight in, the necessary annihilation of all their most favourite indulgences and enjoyments which are contrary to the rule of the Gospel? Let us not suppose that any exhortations will induce such men to change their conduct; they confess the worth of the soul, their obligation to obey, and their peril if they do not; yet, for all this, the present sacrifice required of them is too much for them. They may be told of their Lord's love for them, His self-denying mercy when on earth, His free gifts, and His long-suffering since; they will not be influenced; and why? because the fault is in their heart; they do not like God's service. *They* know full well what they would have, if they might choose. Christ is said to have done all things for us; " Far from it," say they, " He is not a Mediator suited to our case. Give life, give holiness, give truth, give a Saviour to deliver from sin; this is not enough: no, *we* want a Saviour to deliver *in* sin. This is our need. It is a small thing to offer us life, if it be in the way of God's commandments; it is a mockery of our hopes to call that a free gift, which is, in fact, a heavy yoke. We want to do nothing at all, and then the gift will be free indeed. If our hearts *must* be changed to fit us for heaven, let them be changed, only let us have no trouble in the work ourselves. Let the change be part of the work done for us; let us literally be clay in the hands of the potter; let us sleep, and dream, and wake in the morning new men; let us have no fear and trembling, no working out salvation, no self-denial. Let Christ suffer, but be it ours to rejoice only. What we wish is, to be at ease; we wish to have every thing our own way; we wish to enjoy both this world and the next; we wish to be happy all at once. If the Gospel promises this, we accept it; but if not, it is but a bondage, it has no persuasiveness, it will receive no acceptance from us." Such is the language of men's hearts, though their tongues do not utter it; language most unthankful, most profane, most sinful.

These reflections I recommend to the serious attention of those who live in neglect of Holy Communion; but, alas! I must not quit the subject without addressing some cautions to those who are in the observance of it. I would that none of us had need of cautions; but the best of us is in warfare, and on his trial, and none of us can be the worse for them. I need not remind you, my brethren, that there is a peril attached to the unworthy reception; for this is the very excuse which many plead for not receiving; but it often happens, as in other matters also, that men have fears when they should not fear, and do not fear when they should fear. A slight consideration will show this; for what is the danger in communicating? that of coming to it, as St. Paul implies, *without* fear. It is evident then, that, in spite of what was just now said, when persons are in danger of receiving it unworthily, they commonly do not really feel their danger; for their very danger consists in their not fearing. If they did truly and religiously fear the blessed Sacrament, so far they would not be in danger of an unworthy reception.

Now it is plain when it is that persons are in danger of receiving it fearlessly and thoughtlessly; not when they receive it for the first time, but when they have often received it, when they are in the habit of receiving it. This is the dangerous time.

When a Christian first comes to Holy Communion, he comes with awe and anxiety. At least, I will not suppose the case of a person so little in earnest about his soul, and so profane, as to despise the ordinance when he first attends it. Perhaps he has no clear doctrinal notion of the sacred rite, but the very title of it, as the Sacrament of his Lord's Body and Blood, suffices to make him serious. Let us believe that he examines himself, and prays for grace to receive the gift worthily; and he feels at the time of celebration and afterwards, that, having bound himself more strictly to a religious life, and received Divine influences, he has more to answer for. But after he has repeated his attendance several times, this fear and reverence wear-away with the novelty. As he begins to be familiar with the words of the prayers, and the order of the Service, so does he both hear and receive with less emotion and solemnity. It is not that he is a worse man than he was at first, but he is exposed to a greater temptation to be profane. He had no deeper religious principle when he first communicated than he has now (probably not so deep), but his want of acquaintance with the Service kept him from irreverence, indifference, and wandering thoughts : but now this accidental safeguard is removed, and as he has not succeeded in acquiring any habitual reverence from former seasons of communicating, and has no clear knowledge of the nature of the Sacrament to warn and check him, he is exposed to his own ordinary hardness of heart and unbelief, in circumstances much more perilous than those in which they are ordinarily displayed. If it is a sin to neglect God in the world, it is a greater sin to neglect Him in church. Now is the time when he is in danger of not discerning the Lord's Body, of receiving the gift of life as a thing of course, without awe, gratitude, and self-abasement. And the more constant he is in his attendance at the sacred rite, the greater will be his risk ; his *risk*, I say ; that is, if he neglects to be jealous over himself, to watch himself narrowly, and to condemn and hate in himself the faintest risings of coldness and irreverence ; for, of course, if he so acts, the less will be his risk, and the greater will be his security that his heart will not betray him. But I speak of those who are not sufficiently aware of their danger, and these are many.

Here, too, let me mention another sin of a similar character into which communicants are apt to fall; *viz.* a forgetfulness, after communicating, that they have communicated. Even when we resist the coldness which frequent communion may occasion, and strive to possess our minds in as profound a seriousness as we felt when the rite was new to us, even then there is often a painful difference between our feelings before we have attended it, and after. We are diligent in preparation, we are careless in retrospect; we dismiss from our memory what we cherished in our expectations; we forget that we ever hoped and feared. But consider; when we have solemn thoughts about Holy Communion only till we have come to it, what does this imply, but that we imagine that we have received the benefit of it once for all, as a thing done and over, and that there is nothing more to seek? This is but a formal way of worshipping; as if we had wiped off a writing which was against us, and there was an end of the matter. But blessed are those servants who are ever expecting Him, who is ever coming to them; whether He come " at even, or at midnight, or at cock-crowing, or in the morning;" whereas those who first come to Him for the gift of grace, and then neglect to wait for its

progressive accomplishment in their hearts, how pro-
fanely they act! it is as if to receive the blessing in
mockery, and then to cast it away. Surely, after so
great a privilege, we ought to behave ourselves as if we
had partaken some Divine food and medicine (if great
things may be compared to ordinary), which, in its own
inscrutable way, and in its own good time, will " prosper
in the thing whereunto God sends it "—the fruit of the
tree of life which Adam forfeited, which had that
virtue in it, that it was put out of his reach in haste,
lest he should take and eat, and live for ever. How
earnest, then, should be our care lest this gracious
treasure which we carry within us should be lost by our
own fault, by the unhealthy excitements, or the listless
indolence, to which our nature invites us! " Quench
not the Spirit," says the Apostle; surely our privilege
is a burden heavy to bear, before it turn to a principle
of life and strength, till Christ be formed in us perfectly; and we the while, what cause have we to watch,
and pray, and fulfil all righteousness, till the day dawn,
and the day-star arise in our hearts!

Nor let us suppose that by once or twice seeking God
in this gracious ordinance, we can secure the gift for
ever: " Seek the Lord and His strength, seek His face
evermore." The bread which comes down from heaven
is like the manna, " *daily* bread," and that " till He
come," till His " kingdom come." In His coming at
the end of the world, all our wishes and prayers rest and

are accomplished; and in His present communion we have a stay and consolation meanwhile, joining together the past and future, reminding us that He has come once, and promising us that He will come again. Who can live any time in the world, pleasant as it may seem on first entering. it, without discovering that it is a weariness, and that if this life is worth any thing, it is because it is the passage to another? It needs no great religion to feel this; it is a self-evident truth to those who have much experience of the world. The only reason why all do not feel it is, that they have not lived long enough to feel it; and those who feel it more than others, have but been thrown into circumstances to feel it more. But while the times wax old, and the colours of earth fade, and the voice of song is brought low, and all kindreds of the earth can but wail and lament, the sons of God lift up their heads, for their salvation draweth nigh. Nature fails, the sun shines not, and the moon is dim, the stars fall from heaven, and the foundations of the round world shake; but the Altar's light burns ever brighter; there are sights there which the many cannot see, and all above the tumults of earth the command is heard to show forth the Lord's death, and the promise that the Lord is coming.

"Happy are the people that are in such a case!" who, when wearied of the things seen, can turn with good hope to the things unseen; yea, "blessed are the people who have the Lord for their God!" "Come unto Me,"

He says, " all ye that labour and are heavy laden, and I will give you rest." Rest is better than toil; peace satisfies, and quietness disappoints not. These are sure goods. Such is the calm of the heavenly Jerusalem, which is the mother of us all; and such is their calm worship, the foretaste of heaven, who for a season shut themselves out from the world, and seek Him in invisible Presence, whom they shall hereafter see face to face.

SERMON XII.

THE GOSPEL FEAST.

JOHN vi. 5.

" When Jesus then lifted up His eyes, and saw a great company come unto Him, He saith unto Philip, Whence shall we buy bread that these may eat."

AFTER these words the Evangelist adds, " And this He said to prove him, for He Himself knew what He would do." Thus, you see, our Lord had secret meanings when He spoke, and did not bring forth openly all His divine sense at once. He knew what He was about to do from the first, but He wished to lead forward His disciples, and to arrest and open their minds, before He instructed them : for all cannot receive His words, and on the blind and deaf the most sacred truths fall without profit.

And thus, throughout the course of His gracious dispensations from the beginning, it may be said that the Author and Finisher of our faith has hid things from us in mercy, and listened to our questionings, while He Himself knew what He was about to do. He has hid, in order afterwards to reveal, that then, on looking back on what He said and did before, we may see in it what at the time we did not see, and thereby see it to more profit. Thus He hid Himself from the disciples as He walked with them to Emmaus: thus Joseph, too, under different and yet similar circumstances, hid himself from his brethren.

With this thought in our minds, surely we seem to see a new and further meaning still, in the narrative before us. Christ spoke of buying bread, when He intended to create or make bread; but did He not, in that bread which He made, intend further that Heavenly bread which is the salvation of our souls?—for He goes on to say, "Labour not for the meat" or food "which perisheth, but for that food which endureth unto everlasting life, which the Son of man shall give unto you." Yes, surely the wilderness is the world, and the Apostles are His priests, and the multitudes are His people; and that feast, so suddenly, so unexpectedly provided, is the Holy Communion. He alone is the same, He the provider of the loaves then, of the heavenly manna now. All other things change, but He remaineth.

And what is that Heavenly Feast which we now are vouchsafed, but in its own turn the earnest and pledge of that future feast in His Father's kingdom, when "the marriage of the Lamb shall come, and His wife hath made herself ready," and "holy Jerusalem cometh down

[VII]   M from God out of heaven," and " blessed shall they be who shall eat bread in the kingdom of God "?

And further, since to that Feast above we do lift up our eyes, though it will not come till the end; and as we do not make remembrance of it once only, but continually, in the sacred rite which foreshadows it; therefore, in like manner, not in the miracle of the loaves only, though in that especially, but in all parts of Scripture, in history, and in precept, and in promise, and in prophecy, is it given us to see the Gospel Feast typified and prefigured, and that immortal and never-failing Supper in the visible presence of the Lamb which will follow upon it at the end. And if they are blessed who shall eat and drink of that table in the kingdom, so too blessed are they who meditate upon it, and hope for it now,—who read Scripture with it in their thoughts, and endeavour to look beneath the veil of the literal text, and to catch a sight of the gleams of heavenly light which are behind it. " Blessed are your eyes, for they see; and your ears, for they hear; for verily I say unto you, that many prophets and righteous men have desired to see those things which ye see, but have not seen them; and to hear those things which ye hear, and have not heard them." " Blessed are they which have not seen, and yet have believed." Blessed they who see in and by believing, and who have, because they doubt not.

Let us, then, at this time of year[1], as is fitting,

[1] Easter.

follow the train of thought thus opened upon us, and, looking back into the Sacred Volume, trace the intimations and promises there given of that sacred and blessed Feast of Christ's Body and Blood which it is our privilege now to enjoy till the end come.

Now the Old Testament, as we know, is full of figures and types of the Gospel; types various, and, in their literal wording, contrary to each other, but all meeting and harmoniously fulfilled in Christ and His Church. Thus the histories of the Israelites in the wilderness, and of the Israelites when settled in Canaan, alike are ours, representing our present state as Christians. Our Christian life is a state of faith and trial; it is also a state of enjoyment. It has the richness of the promised land; it has the marvellousness of the desert. It is a "good land, a land of brooks of water, of fountains and depths that spring out of vallies and hills; a land of wheat and barley, and vines, and fig-trees, and pomegranates; a land of oil olive, and honey; a land wherein thou shalt eat bread without scarceness; thou shalt not lack any thing in it; a land whose stones are iron, and out of whose hills thou mayest dig brass." And, on the other hand, it is still a land which to the natural man seems a wilderness, a "great and terrible wilderness, wherein are fiery serpents, and scorpions, and drought, where there is no water;" where faith is still necessary, and where, still more forcibly than in the case of Israel, the maxim holds, that "man doth not live by bread only, but by every word that pro-ceedeth out of the mouth of the Lord doth man live."

This is the state in which we are,—a state of faith and of possession. In the desert the Israelites lived by the signs of things, without the realities : manna was to stand for the corn, oil, and honey, of the good land promised; water, for the wine and milk. It was a time for faith to exercise itself; and when they came into the promised land, then was the time of possession. That was the land of milk and honey; they needed not any divinely provided compensations or expedients. Manna was not needed, nor the pillar of the cloud, nor the water from the rock. But we Christians, on the con-trary, are at once in the wilderness and in the promised land. In the wilderness, because we live amid wonders; in the promised land, because we are in a state of enjoy-ment. That we are in the state of enjoyment is surely certain, unless all the prophecies have failed; and that we are in a state in which faith alone has that enjoy-ment, is plain from the fact that God's great blessings are not seen, and in that the Apostle says, "We walk by faith, not by sight." In a word, we are in a super-natural state,—a word which implies both its greatness and its secretness : for what is above nature, is at once not seen, and is more precious than what is seen; "the things which are seen are temporal, the things which are not seen are eternal."

And if our state altogether is parallel to that of the

Israelites, as an antitype to its type, it is natural to think that so great a gift as Holy Communion would not be without its appropriate figures and symbols in the Old Testament. All that our Saviour has done is again and again shadowed out in the Old Testament; and this, therefore, it is natural to think, as well as other things : His miraculous birth, His life, His teaching, His death, His priesthood, His sacrifice, His resurrection, His glorification, His kingdom, are again and again prefigured : it is not reasonable to suppose that if this so great gift is really given us, it should be omitted. He who died for us, is He who feeds us; and as His death is mentioned, so we may beforehand expect will be mentioned the feast He gives us. Not openly indeed, for neither is His death nor His priesthood taught openly, but covertly, under the types of David or Aaron, or other favoured servants of God; and in like manner we might expect, and we shall find, the like reverent allusions to His most gracious Feast,—allusions which we should not know to *be* allusions but for the event; just as we should not know that Solomon, Aaron, or Samuel, stood for Christ at all, except that the event explains the figure. When Abraham said to Isaac, " God will provide Himself a lamb for a burnt offering," who can doubt this is a prophecy concerning Christ?—yet we are nowhere told it in Scripture. The case is the same as regards the Sacrament of Baptism. Now that it is given, we cannot doubt that the purifications of the Jews, Naaman's bathing, and the prophecy of a fountain being opened for sin and all uncleanness, have reference to it, as being the visible fulfilment of the great spiritual cleansing : and St. Peter expressly affirms this of the Deluge, and St. Paul of the passage of the Red Sea. And in like manner passages in the Bible, which speak prophetically of the Gospel Feast, cannot but refer (if I may so speak) to the Holy Sacrament of the Lord's Supper, as being, in fact, the Feast given us under the Gospel.

And let it be observed, directly we know that we have this great gift, and that the Old Testament history prefigures it, we have a light thrown upon what otherwise is a difficulty; for, it may be asked with some speciousness, whether the Jews were not in a higher state of privilege than we Christians, until we take this gift into account. It may be objected that our blessings are all future or distant,—the hope of eternal life, which is to be fulfilled hereafter, God's forgiveness, who is in heaven: what do we gain now and here above the Jews? God loved the Jews, and He *gave* them something; He gave them present gifts; the Old Testament is full of the description of them; He gave them "the precious things of heaven, and the dew, and the deep that coucheth beneath, and precious things brought forth by the sun, and by the moon, and the chief things of the ancient mountains, and the precious things of the lasting hills, and the precious things of the earth, and

the fulness thereof," " honey out of the rock, and oil out
of the flinty rock, butter of kine, and milk of sheep,
with fat of lambs, and rams of the breed of Bashan, and
goats, with the fat of kidneys of wheat, and the pure
blood of the grape [1]." These were present real blessings.
What has He given *us* ?—*nothing* in possession ? *all* in
promise ? This, I say, is in itself not likely ; it is not
likely that He should so reverse His system, and make
the Gospel inferior to the Law. But the knowledge of
the great gift under consideration clears up this per-
plexity ; for every passage in the Old Testament which
speaks of the temporal blessings given by God to His ancient people, instead of conveying to us a painful sense of
destitution, and exciting our jealousy, reminds us of our
greater blessedness ; for every passage which belongs to
them is fulfilled now in a higher sense to us. We have
no need to envy them. God did not take away their
blessings, without giving us greater. The Law was
not so much taken away, as the Gospel given. The
Gospel supplanted the Law. The Law went out by the
Gospel's coming in. Only our blessings are not seen ;
therefore they are higher, *because* they are unseen.
Higher blessings could not be visible. How could spiritual blessings be visible ones ? If Christ now feeds us,
not with milk and honey, but " with the spiritual food
of His most precious Body and Blood ;" if " our sinful
bodies are made clean by His Body, and our souls

[1] Deut. xxxii. 13 ; xxxiii. 13—15.

washed through His most precious Blood," truly we are not without our precious things, any more than Israel was: but they are unseen, because so much greater, so spiritual; they are given only under the veil of what is seen: and thus we Christians are both with the Church in the wilderness as regards faith, and in the Church in Canaan as regards enjoyment; having the fulfilment of the words spoken by Moses, repeated by our Lord, to which I just now referred, "Man shall not live by bread only, but by every word which proceedeth out of the mouth of God."

Now, then, I will refer to some passages of both the Old Testament and the New, which both illustrate and are illustrated by this great doctrine of the Gospel.

1. And, first, let it be observed, from the beginning, the greatest rite of religion has been a feast; the partaking of God's bounties, in the way of nature, has been consecrated to a more immediate communion with God Himself. For instance, when Isaac was weaned, Abraham "made a great feast [1]," and then it was that Sarah prophesied; "Cast out this bondwoman and her son," she said, prophesying the introduction of the spirit, grace, and truth, which the Gospel contains, instead of the bondage of the outward forms of the Law. Again, it was at a feast of savoury meat that the spirit of prophecy came upon Isaac, and he blessed Jacob. In like manner the first beginning of our Lord's miracles was at

[1] Gen. xxi. 10.

a marriage feast, when He changed water into wine; and when St. Matthew was converted he entertained our Lord at a feast. At a feast, too, our Lord allowed the penitent woman to wash with tears and anoint His feet, and pronounced her forgiveness; and at a feast, before His passion, He allowed Mary to anoint them with costly ointment, and to wipe them with her hair. Thus with our Lord, and with the Patriarchs, a feast was a time of grace; so much so, that He was said by the Pharisees to come eating and drinking, to be "a winebibber and gluttonous, a friend of publicans and sinners [1]."

2. And next, in order to make this feasting still more solemn, it had been usual at all times to precede it by a direct act of religion,—by a prayer, or blessing, or sacrifice, or by the presence of a priest, which implied it. Thus, when Melchizedek came out to meet Abraham, and *bless* him, "he brought forth bread and wine [2];" to which it is added, "and he was the priest of the Most High God." Such, too, was the lamb of the Passover, which was eaten roast with fire, and with unleavened bread, and bitter herbs, with girded loins and shoes on, and staff in hand; as the Lord's Passover, being a solemn religious feast, even if not a sacrifice. And such seems to have been the common notion of communion with God all the world over, however it was gained; *viz.* that we arrived at the possession of His

[1] Matt. xi. 19. Luke vii. 34. [2] Gen. xiv. 18.

invisible gifts by participation in His visible; that there was some mysterious connexion between the seen and the unseen; and that, by setting aside the choicest of His earthly bounties, as a specimen and representative of the whole, presenting it to Him for His blessing, and then taking, eating, and appropriating it, we had the best hope of gaining those unknown and indefinite gifts which human nature needs. This the heathen practised towards their idols also; and St. Paul seems to acknowledge that in that way they did communicate, though most miserably and fearfully, with those idols, and with the evil spirits which they represented. "The things which the Gentiles sacrifice, they sacrifice to devils, and not to God; and I would not that ye should hold communion with devils [1]." Here, as before, a feast is spoken of as the means of communicating with the unseen world, though, when the feast was idolatrous, it was the fellowship of evil spirits.

3. And next let this be observed, that the descriptions in the Old Testament of the perfect state of religious privilege, *viz.* that under the Gospel which was then to come, are continually made under the image of a feast, a feast of some special and choice goods of this world, corn, wine, and the like; goods of this world chosen from the mass as a specimen of all, as types and means of seeking, and means of obtaining, the unknown spiritual blessings, which "eye hath not seen nor ear

[1] 1 Cor. x. 20.

heard." And these special goods of nature, so set apart, are more frequently than any thing else, corn or bread, and wine, as the figures of what was greater, though others are mentioned also. Now the first of these of which we read is the fruit of the tree of life, the leaves of which are also mentioned in the prophets. The tree of life was that tree in the garden of Eden, the eating of which would have made Adam immortal; a divine gift lay hid in an outward form. The prophet Ezekiel speaks of it afterwards in the following words, showing that a similar blessing was in store for the redeemed :— "By the river, upon the bank thereof, on this side, and on that side, shall grow all trees for meat, whose leaf shall not fade, neither shall the fruit thereof be consumed. It shall bring forth new fruits according to his months, because their waters they issued out of the sanctuary; and the fruit thereof shall be for meat, and the leaf thereof for medicine[1]." Like to which is St. John's account of the tree of life, "which bare twelve manner of fruits, and yielded her fruit every month; and the leaves of the tree were for the healing of the nations[2]." And hence we read in the Canticles of the apple-tree, and of sitting down under its shadow, and its fruit being sweet to the taste. Here then in type is signified the sacred gift of which I am speaking; and yet it has not seemed good to the gracious Giver literally to select fruit or leaves as the means of His

[1] Ezek. xlvii. 12. [2] Rev. xxii. 2.

invisible blessings. He might have spiritually fed us with such, had He pleased—for man liveth not by bread only, but by the word of His mouth. His Word might have made the fruit of the tree His Sacrament, but He has willed otherwise.

The next selection of gifts of the earth which we find in Scripture, is the very one which He at length fixed on, bread and wine, as in the history of Melchizedek; and there the record stands as a prophecy of what was to be: for who is Melchizedek but our Lord and Saviour, and what is the Bread and Wine but the very feast which He has ordained?

Next the great gift was shadowed out in the description of the promised land, which was said to flow with milk and honey, and in all those other precious things of nature which I have already recounted as belonging to the promised land, oil, butter, corn, wine, and the like. These all may be considered to refer to the Gospel feast typically, because they were the rarest and most exquisite of the blessings given to the Jews, as the Gospel Feast is the most choice and most sacred of all the blessings given to us Christians; and what is most precious under the one Dispensation is signified by what is most precious under the other.

Now let us proceed to the Prophets, and we shall find the like anticipation of the Gospel Feast.

For instance, you recollect, the prophet Hosea says: "It shall come to pass in that day, I will hear, saith the Lord,

I will hear the heavens, and they shall hear the earth, and the earth shall hear the corn, and the wine, and the oil, and they shall hear Jezreel. And I will sow her unto Me in the earth[1]." By Jezreel is meant the Christian Church; and the Prophet declares in God's name, that the time was to come when the Church would call upon the corn, wine, and oil, and they would call on the earth, and the earth on the heavens, and the heavens on God; and God should answer the heavens, and the heavens should answer the earth, and the earth should answer the corn, wine, and oil, and they should answer to the wants of the Church. Now, doubtless, this may be fulfilled only in a general way; but considering Almighty God has appointed corn or bread, and wine, to be the special instruments of His ineffable grace,—He, who sees the end from the beginning, and who views all things in all their relations at once,—He, when He spoke of corn and wine, knew that the word would be fulfilled, not generally only, but even literally in the Gospel.

Again: the prophet Joel says, "It shall come to pass in that day that the mountains shall drop down new wine, and the hills shall flow with milk, and all the rivers of Judah shall flow with waters, and a fountain shall come forth of the house of the Lord, and shall water the valley of Shittim[2]." How strikingly is this fulfilled, if we take it to apply to what God has given us in the Gospel, in the feast of the Holy Communion!

[1] Hos. ii. 21—23.   [2] Joel iii. 18.

Again: the prophet Amos says: "Behold, the days come, saith the Lord, when the plowman shall overtake the reaper, and the treader of grapes him that soweth seed; and the mountains shall drop sweet wine, and all the hills shall melt[1];" that is, with God's marvellous grace, whereby He gives us gifts new and wonderful.

And the prophet Isaiah: "In this mountain shall the Lord of Hosts make unto all people a feast of fat things, a feast of wines on the lees; of fat things full of marrow, of wines on the lees well refined." And again: "Surely I will no more give thy corn to be meat for thine enemies, and the sons of the stranger shall not drink thy wine, for the which thou hast laboured; but they that have gathered it shall eat it, and praise the Lord, and they that have brought it together shall drink it in the courts of My holiness." And again: "Behold My servants shall eat, but ye shall be hungry; behold My servants shall drink, but ye shall be thirsty[2]."

Again: the prophet Jeremiah says: "They shall come and sing in the height of Zion, and shall flow together to the goodness of the Lord, for wheat, and for wine, and for oil, and for the young of the flock and of the herd; and their soul shall be as a watered garden, and they shall not sorrow any more at all . . . And I will satiate the soul of the priests with fatness, and My people shall be satisfied with My goodness, saith the Lord[3]."

---

[1] Amos ix. 13. [2] Isa. xxv. 6; lxii. 8, 9; lxv. 13.
[3] Jer. xxxi. 12—14.

And the prophet Zechariah: "How great is His goodness, and how great is His beauty! corn shall make the young men cheerful, and new wine the maids[1]."

And under a different image, but with the same general sense, the prophet Malachi: "From the rising of the sun even unto the going down of the same, My Name shall be great among the Gentiles; and in every place incense shall be offered unto My Name, and a pure offering, for My Name shall be great among the heathen, saith the Lord of Hosts[2]."

Further, if the Psalms are intended for Christian worship, as surely they are, the Prophetic Spirit, who inspired them, saw that they too would in various places describe that sacred Christian feast, which we feel they do describe; and surely we may rightly call this coincidence between the ordinance in the Christian Church and the form of words in the Psalms, a mark of design. For instance: "Thou shalt prepare a Table before me against them that trouble me. Thou hast anointed my head with oil, and my Cup shall be full." "I will wash my hands in innocency, O Lord, and so will I go to Thine Altar." "O send out Thy light and Thy truth, that they may lead me, and bring me unto Thy holy hill, and to Thy dwelling; and that I may go unto the Altar of God, even unto the God of my joy and gladness." "The children of men shall put their trust under the shadow of Thy wings. They shall be satisfied

[1] Zech. ix. 17.   [2] Mal. i. 11.

with the plenteousness of Thy house, and Thou shalt give them drink of Thy pleasures as out of the river. For with Thee is the well of. life, and in Thy light shall we see light." "Blessed is the man whom Thou choosest and receivest unto Thee; he shall dwell in Thy court, and shall be satisfied with the pleasures of Thy house, even of Thy Holy Temple." "My soul shall be satisfied, even as it were with marrow and fatness, when my mouth praiseth Thee with joyful lips ... because Thou hast been my helper, therefore under the shadow of Thy wings will I rejoice[1]."

The same wonderful feast is put before us in the book of Proverbs, where Wisdom stands for Christ. "Wisdom hath builded her house," that is, Christ has built His Church; "she hath hewn out her seven pillars, she hath killed her beasts, she hath mingled her wine (that is, Christ has prepared His Supper), she hath also furnished her table (that is, the Lord's Table), she hath sent forth her maidens (that is, the priests of the Lord), she crieth upon the highest places of the city, Whoso is simple, let him turn in hither; as for him that wanteth understanding, she saith to him, Come, eat of My Bread and drink of the Wine which I have mingled[2]," —which is like saying, "Come unto Me all ye that labour and are heavy laden and I will refresh you." Like which are the prophet Isaiah's words: "Ho, every

[1] Ps. xxiii. 5; xxvi. 6; xxxvi. 7—9; xliii. 3, 4; lxv. 4; lxiii. 6—8.
[2] Prov. ix. 1—5.

one that thirsteth, come ye to the waters, and he that hath no money, come ye buy and eat; yea, come, buy wine and milk without money and without price[1]." And such too is the description in the book of Canticles : " The fig tree putteth forth her green figs, and the vines with the tender grapes give a good smell" . . . . " Until the day break and the shadows flee away, I will get me to the mountain of myrrh, and to the hill of frankincense" . . . "I have gathered My myrrh with My spice, I have eaten My honeycomb with My honey, I have drunk My wine with My milk; eat, O friends, drink, yea drink abundantly, O beloved[2]!" In connexion with such passages as these should be observed St. Paul's words, which seem from the antithesis to be an allusion to the same most sacred Ordinance : " Be not drunk with wine, wherein is excess, but be filled with the Spirit," with that new wine which God the Holy Spirit ministers in the Supper of the Great King.

God grant that we may be able ever to come to this Blessed Sacrament with feelings suitable to the passages which I have read concerning it ! May we not regard it in a cold, heartless way, and keep at a distance from fear, when we should rejoice ! May the spirit of the unprofitable servant never be ours, who looked at his lord as a hard master instead of a gracious benefactor ! May we not be in the number of those who go on year after year, and never approach Him at all ! May we

[1] Isa. lv. 1.   [2] Cant. ii. 13; iv. 6; v. 1.

not be of those who went, one to his farm, another to his merchandise, when they were called to the wedding! Nor let us be of those, who come in a formal, mechanical way, as a mere matter of obligation, without reverence, without awe, without wonder, without love. Nor let us fall into the sin of those who complained that they have nothing to gather but the manna, wearying of God's gifts.

But let us come in faith and hope, and let us say to ourselves, May this be the beginning to us of everlasting bliss!   May these be the first fruits of that banquet which is to last for ever and ever; ever new, ever transporting, inexhaustible, in the city of our God!

SERMON XIII.

LOVE OF RELIGION, A NEW NATURE.

ROMANS vi. 8.

"If we be dead with Christ, we believe that we shall also live with Him."

TO be dead with Christ, is to hate and turn from sin; and to live with Him, is to have our hearts and minds turned towards God and Heaven. To be dead to sin, is to feel a disgust at it. We know what is meant by disgust. Take, for instance, the case of a sick man, when food of a certain kind is presented to him,—and there is no doubt what is meant by disgust. Consider how certain scents, which are too sweet or too strong, or certain tastes, affect certain persons under certain circumstances, or always,—and you will be at no loss to determine what is meant by disgust at sin, or deadness to sin. On the other hand, consider how pleasant a meal is to the hungry, or some enlivening odour to the faint; how refreshing the air is to the languid, or the brook to the weary and thirsty;—and you will understand the sort of feeling which is implied in being alive with Christ, alive to religion, alive to the thought of heaven. Our animal powers cannot exist in all atmospheres; certain airs are poisonous, others life-giving. So is it with spirits and souls: an unrenewed spirit could not live in heaven, he would die; an Angel could not live in hell. The natural man cannot live in heavenly company, and the angelic soul would pine and waste away in the company of sinners, unless God's sacred presence were continued to it. To be dead to sin, is to be so minded, that the atmosphere of sin (if I may so speak) oppresses, distresses, and stifles us,—that it is painful and unnatural to us to remain in it. To be alive with Christ, is to be so minded, that the atmosphere of heaven refreshes, enlivens, stimulates, invigorates us. To be alive, is not merely to bear the thought of religion, to assent to the truth of religion, to wish to be religious; but to be drawn towards it, to love it, to delight in it, to obey it. Now I suppose most persons called Christians do not go farther than this,—to wish to be religious, and to think it right to be religious, and to feel a respect for religious men; they do not get so far as to have any sort of love for religion.

So far, however, they do go; not, indeed, to do their duty and to love it, but to have a sort of wish that they did. I suppose there are few persons but, at the very least, now and then feel the wish to be holy and religious. They bear witness to the excellence of virtuous and holy living, they consent to all that their teachers tell them, what they hear in church, and read in religious books; but all this is a very different thing from acting according to their knowledge. They confess one thing, they do another.

Nay, they confess one thing *while* they do another. Even sinners,—wilful, abandoned sinners,—if they would be honest enough to speak as they really in their hearts feel, would own, while they are indulging in the pleasures of sin, while they idle away the Lord's Day, or while they keep bad company, or while they lie or cheat, or while they drink to excess, or do any other bad thing,—they would confess, I say, did they speak their minds, that it is a far happier thing, even at present, to live in obedience to God, than in obedience to Satan. Not that sin has not its pleasures, such as they are; I do not mean, of course, to deny that,—I do not deny that Satan is able to give us something in exchange for future and eternal happiness; I do not say that irreligious men do not gain pleasures, which religious men are obliged to lose. I know they do; if they did not, there would be nothing to tempt and try us. But, after all, the pleasures which the servants of Satan enjoy, though pleasant, are always attended with pain too; with a bitterness, which, though it does not destroy the pleasure, yet is by itself sufficient to make it far less pleasant, even while it lasts, than such pleasures as are without such bitterness, viz. the pleasures of religion. This, then, alas! is the state of multitudes; not to be dead to sin and alive to God, but, while they are alive to sin and the world, to have just so much sense of heaven, as not to be able to enjoy either.

I say, when any one, man or woman, young or old, is conscious that he or she is going wrong, whether in greater matter or less, whether in not coming to church when there is no good excuse, neglecting private prayer, living carelessly, or indulging in known sin,—this bad conscience is from time to time a torment to such persons. For a little while, perhaps, they do not feel it, but then the pain comes on again. It is a keen, harassing, disquieting, hateful pain, which hinders sinners from being happy. They *may* have pleasures, but they cannot be *happy*. They know that God is angry with them; and they know that, at some time or other, He will visit, He will judge, He will punish. They try to get this out of their minds, but the arrow sticks fast there; it keeps its hold. They try to laugh it off, or to be bold and daring, or to be angry and violent. They are loud or unkind in their answers to those, who remind them of it either in set words, or by their example. But it keeps its hold. And so it is, that all men who are not very abandoned, bad men as well as good, wish that they were holy as God is holy, pure as Christ was pure, even though they do not try to be, or pray to God to make them, holy and pure; not that they *like* religion, but that they know, they are convinced in their reason, they feel sure, that religion alone is happiness.

Oh, what a dreadful state, to have our desires one way, and our knowledge and conscience another; to have our life, our breath and food, upon the earth, and our eyes upon Him who died once and now liveth; to look upon Him who once was pierced, yet not to rise with Him and live with Him; to feel that a holy life is our only happiness, yet to have no heart to pursue it; to be certain that the wages of sin is death, yet to practise sin; to confess that the Angels alone are perfectly happy, for they do God's will perfectly, yet to prepare ourselves for nothing else but the company of devils; to acknowledge that Christ is our only hope, yet deliberately to let that hope go! O miserable state! miserable they, if any there are who now hear me, who are thus circumstanced!

At first sight, it might seem impossible that any such persons could be found in church. At first sight, one might be tempted to say, " All who come to church, at least, are in earnest, and have given up sin; they are imperfect indeed, as all Christians are at best, but they do not fall into wilful sin." I should be very glad, my Brethren, to believe this were the case, but I cannot indulge so pleasant a hope. No; I think it quite certain that some persons at least, I do not say how many, to whom I am speaking, have not made up their minds fully to lead a religious life. They come to church because they think it right, or from other cause. It is very right that they should come; I am glad they do.

This is good, as far as it goes; but it is not all. They are not so far advanced in the kingdom of God, as to resist the devil, or to flee from him. They cannot command themselves. They act rightly one day, and wrongly the next. They are afraid of being laughed at. They are attracted by bad company. They put off religion to a future day. They think a religious life dull and unpleasant. Yet they have a certain sense of religion; and they come to church in order to satisfy this sense. Now, I say it is right to come to church; but, O that they could be persuaded of the simple truth of St. Paul's words, "He is not a Jew which is one outwardly; but he is a Jew which is one inwardly; and circumcision is that of the heart in the spirit, and not in the letter, whose praise is not of men, but of God [1];" which may be taken to mean :—He is not a Christian who is one outwardly, who merely comes to church, and professes to desire to be saved by Christ. It is very right that he should do so, but it is not enough. He is not a Christian who merely has not cast off religion; but he is the true Christian, who, while he is a Christian outwardly, is one inwardly also; who lives to God; whose secret life is hid with Christ in God; whose heart is religious; who not only knows and feels that a religious life is true happiness, but loves religion, wishes, tries, prays to be religious, begs God Almighty to give him the will and the power to be religious; and,

[1] Rom. ii. 28, 29.

as time goes on, grows more and more religious, more fit for heaven.

We can do nothing right, unless God gives us the will and the power; we cannot please Him without the aid of His Holy Spirit. If any one does not deeply feel this as a first truth in religion, he is preparing for himself a dreadful fall. He will attempt, and he will fail signally, utterly. His own miserable experience will make him sure of it, if he will not believe it, as Scripture declares it. But it is not unlikely that some persons, perhaps some who now hear me, may fall into an opposite mistake. They may attempt to excuse their lukewarmness and sinfulness, on the plea that God does not inwardly move them; and they may argue that those holy men whom they so much admire, those saints who are to sit on Christ's right and left, are of different nature from themselves, sanctified from their mother's womb, visited, guarded, renewed, strengthened, enlightened in a peculiar way, so as to make it no wonder that they *are* saints, and no fault that they themselves are not. But this is not so; let us not thus miserably deceive ourselves. St. Paul says expressly of himself and the other Apostles, that they were " men of like passions " with the poor ignorant heathen to whom they preached. And does not his history show this? Do you not recollect what he was before his conversion? Did he not rage like a beast of prey against the disciples of Christ? and how was he converted? by the vision of our Lord? Yes, in one sense, but not by it alone; hear his own words, "Whereupon, O King Agrippa, I was not *disobedient* unto the heavenly vision." His obedience was necessary for his conversion; he could not obey without grace; but he would have received grace in vain, had he not obeyed. And, afterwards, was he at once perfect? No; for he says expressly, "not as though I had already attained, either were already perfect;" and elsewhere he tells us that he had a "thorn in the flesh, the messenger of Satan to buffet him;" and he was obliged to "bruise his body and bring it into subjection, lest, after he had preached to others, he should be himself a castaway." St. Paul conquered, as any one of us must conquer, by "striving," struggling, "to enter in at the strait gate;" he "wrought out his salvation with fear and trembling," as we must do.

This is a point which must be insisted on for the encouragement of the fearful, the confutation of the hypocritical, and the abasement of the holy. In this world, even the best of men, though they are dead to sin, and have put sin to death, yet have that dead and corrupt thing within them, though they live to God; they have still an enemy of God remaining in their hearts, though they keep it in subjection. This, indeed, is what all men now have in common, a root of evil in them, a principle of sin, or what may become such;— what they differ in is this, not that one man has it, another not; but that one lives in and to it, another not;

one subdues it, another not. A holy man is by nature subject to sin equally with others; but he is holy because he subdues, tramples on, chains up, imprisons, puts out of the way this law of sin, and is ruled by religious and spiritual motives. Of Christ alone can it be said that He " did no sin, neither was guile found in His mouth." The prince of this world came and found nothing in Him. He had no root of sin in His heart; He was not born in Adam's sin. Far different are we. He was thus pure, because He was the Son of God, and born of a Virgin. But we are conceived in sin and shapen in iniquity. And since that which is born of the flesh, is flesh, we are sinful and corrupt because we are sinfully begotten of sinners. Even those then who in the end turn out to be saints and attain to life eternal, yet are not born saints, but have with God's regenerating and renewing grace to make themselves saints. It is nothing but the Cross of Christ, without us and within us, which changes any one of us from being (as I may say) a devil, into an Angel. We are all by birth children of wrath. We are at best like good olive trees, which have become good by being grafted on a good tree. By nature we are like wild trees, bearing sour and bitter fruit, and so we should remain, were we not grafted upon Christ, the good olive tree, made members of Christ, the righteous and holy and well-beloved Son of God. Hence it is that there is such a change in a saint of God from what he was at the first.   Consider what a different man St. Paul was after his conversion and before,—raging, as I just now said, like some wild beast, with persecuting fury against the Church, before Christ appeared to him, and meekly suffering persecution and glorying in it afterwards. Think of St. Peter denying Christ before the resurrection, and confessing, suffering, and dying for Him afterwards.   And so now many an aged saint, who has good hope of heaven, may recollect things of himself when young, which fill him with dismay.   I do not speak as if God's saints led vicious and immoral lives when young ; but I mean that their lower and evil nature was not subdued, and perhaps from time to time broke out and betrayed them into deeds and words so very different from what is seen in them at present, that did their friends know of them what they themselves know, they would not think them the same persons, and would be quite overpowered with astonishment.   We never can guess what a man is by nature, by seeing what self-discipline has made him.   Yet if we do become thereby changed and prepared for heaven, it is no praise or merit to us.   It is God's doing—glory be to Him, who has wrought so wonderfully with us !   Yet in this life, even to the end, there will be enough evil in us to humble us ; even to the end, the holiest men have remains and stains of sin which they would fain get rid of, if they could, and which keep this life from being to them, for all God's grace, a heaven upon earth.   No, the Christian life is but a shadow of heaven. Its festal and holy days are but shadows of eternity. But hereafter it will be otherwise. In heaven, sin will be utterly destroyed in every elect soul. We shall have no earthly wishes, no tendencies to disobedience or irreligion, no love of the world or the flesh, to draw us off from supreme devotion to God. We shall have our Saviour's holiness fulfilled in us, and be able to love God without drawback or infirmity.

That indeed will be a full reward of all our longings here, to praise and serve God eternally with a single and perfect heart in the midst of His Temple. What a time will that be, when all will be perfected in us which at present is but feebly begun! Then we shall see how the Angels worship God. We shall see the calmness, the intenseness, the purity, of their worship. We shall see that awful sight, the Throne of God, and the Seraphim before and around it, crying, "Holy!" We attempt now to imitate in church what there is performed, as in the beginning, and ever shall be. In the Te Deum, day by day we say, "Holy, Holy, Holy, Lord God of Sabaoth." In the Creed, we recount God's mercies to us sinners. And we say and sing Psalms and Hymns, to come as near heaven as we can. May these attempts of ours be blest by Almighty God, to prepare us for Him! may they be, not dead forms, but living services, living with life from God the Holy Ghost, in those who are dead to sin and who live with

Christ! I dare say some of you have heard persons, who dissent from the Church, say (at any rate, they do say), that our Prayers and Services, and Holy days, are only forms, dead forms, which can do us no good. Yes, they are dead forms to those who are dead, but they are living forms to those who are living. If you come here in a dead way, not in faith, not coming for a blessing, without your hearts being in the service, you will get no benefit from it. But if you come in a living way, in faith, and hope, and reverence, and with holy expectant hearts, then all that takes place will be a living service and full of heaven.

Make use, then, of this Holy Easter Season, which lasts forty to fifty days, to become more like Him who died for you, and who now liveth for evermore. He promises us, " Because I live, ye shall live also." He, by dying on the Cross, opened the Kingdom of Heaven to all believers. He first died, and then He opened heaven. We, therefore, first commemorate His death, and then, for some weeks in succession, we commemorate and show forth the joys of heaven. They who do not rejoice in the weeks after Easter, would not rejoice in heaven itself. These weeks are a sort of beginning of heaven. Pray God to enable you to rejoice; to enable you to keep the Feast duly. Pray God to make you better Christians. This world is a dream,—you will get no good from it. Perhaps you find this difficult to believe; but be sure so it is. Depend upon it, at the

last, you will confess it. Young people expect good
from the world, and people of middle age devote themselves to it, and even old people do not like to give it
up. But the world is your enemy, and the flesh is your
enemy. Come to God, and beg of Him grace to devote
yourselves to Him. Beg of Him the will to follow
Him; beg of Him the power to obey Him. O how
comfortable, pleasant, sweet, soothing, and satisfying
is it to lead a holy life,—the life of Angels! It is
difficult at first; but with God's grace, all things are
possible. O how pleasant to have done with sin! how
good and joyful to flee temptation and to resist evil!
how meet, and worthy, and fitting, and right, to die
unto sin, and to live unto righteousness!

SERMON XIV.

RELIGION PLEASANT TO THE RELIGIOUS.

PSALM xxxiv. 8.

" O taste and see how gracious the Lord is: blessed is the man that trusteth in Him."

YOU see by these words what love Almighty God has towards us, and what claims He has upon our love. He is the Most High, and All-Holy. He inhabiteth eternity : we are but worms compared with Him. He would not be less happy though He had never created us ; He would not be less happy though we were all blotted out again from creation. But He is the God of love ; He brought us all into existence, because He found satisfaction in surrounding Himself with happy creatures : He made us innocent, holy, upright, and happy. And when Adam fell into sin and his descendants after him, then ever since He has been imploring us to return to Him, the Source of all good, by true repentance. "Turn ye, turn ye," He says, "why will ye die ? As I live I have no pleasure in the death of the wicked." "What could have been done more to My vineyard that I have not done to it [1]?" And in the text He condescends to invite us to Him : " O taste and see how gracious the Lord is : blessed is the man that trusteth in Him." As if He said, "If you would but make trial, one trial, if you would but be persuaded to taste and judge for yourself, so excellent is His graciousness, that you would never cease to desire, never cease to approach Him :" according to the saying of the wise man, " They that eat Me shall yet be hungry, and they that drink Me shall yet be thirsty [2]."

This excellence and desirableness of God's gifts is a subject again and again set before us in Holy Scripture. Thus the Prophet Isaiah speaks of the " feast of fat things, a feast of wines on the lees; of fat things full of marrow, of wines on the lees well refined [3]." And again, under images of another kind : " He hath sent Me . . . to give . . . . beauty for ashes, the oil of joy for mourning, the garment of praise for the spirit of heaviness, that they may be called Trees of Righteousness [4]." Or again, the Prophet Hosea : " I will be as the dew unto Israel : he shall grow as the lily, and cast forth his roots as Lebanon. His branches shall spread, and his beauty shall be as the olive-tree, and his smell as Lebanon. They that dwell under his shadow shall return ; they shall revive as the corn, and grow as the vine : the scent thereof shall be as the wine of Leba-

---

[1] Ezek. xxxiii. 11. Isa. v. 4.   [2] Ecclus. xxiv. 21.
[3] Isa. xxv. 6.   [4] Isa. lxi. 1—3.

non [1]." And the Psalmist: "O that My people would have hearkened unto Me . . . . the haters of the Lord should have been found liars, but their time should have endured for ever. He should have fed them also with the finest wheat flour, and with honey out of the stony rock should I have satisfied thee [2]." You see all images of what is pleasant and sweet in nature are brought together to describe the pleasantness and sweetness of the gifts which God gives us in grace. As wine enlivens, and bread strengthens, and oil is rich, and honey is sweet, and flowers are fragrant, and dew is refreshing, and foliage is beautiful; so, and much more, are God's gifts in the Gospel enlivening, and strengthening, and rich, and sweet, and fragrant, and refreshing, and excellent. And as it is natural to feel satisfaction and comfort in these gifts of the visible world, so it is but natural and necessary to be delighted and transported with the gifts of the world invisible; and as the visible gifts are objects of desire and search, so much more is it, I do not merely say a duty, but a privilege and blessedness to "taste and see how gracious the Lord is."

Other passages in the Psalms speak of this blessedness, besides the text. "Thou hast put gladness in my heart," says the Psalmist, "since the time that their corn and wine and oil increased [3]." "The lot is fallen

---

[1] Hos. xiv. 5—7. [2] Ps. lxxxi. 13—16.

[3] Ps. iv. 7.

unto me in a fair ground, yea, I have a goodly heritage[1]." Again, "The statutes of the Lord are right,
and rejoice the heart, . . . more to be desired are they
than gold, yea, than much fine gold, sweeter also than
honey and the honeycomb[2]." "My heart trusted in
Him, and I am helped; therefore my heart danceth for
joy, and in my song will I praise Him[3]." Once more:
"Blessed is the man whom Thou choosest and receivest
unto Thee: he shall dwell in Thy courts, and shall be
satisfied with the pleasures of Thy house, even of Thy
holy temple[4]."

I wish it were possible, my brethren, to lead men to
greater holiness and more faithful obedience by setting
before them the high and abundant joys which they
have who serve God: "In His presence is fulness of
joy," "the well of life;" and they are satisfied with
"the plenteousness of His house," and "drink of His
pleasures as out of a river;" but this is, I know, just
what most persons will not believe. They think that it
is very right and proper to be religious; they think that
it would be better for themselves in the world to come
if they were religious now. They do not at all deny
either the duty or the expedience of leading a new and
holy life; but they cannot understand how it can be
pleasant: they cannot believe or admit that it is more
pleasant than a life of liberty, laxity, and enjoyment

---

[1] Ps. xvi. 6.
[2] Ps. xix. 10.
[3] Ps. xxviii. 7.
[4] Ps. lxv. 4.

They, as it were, say, " Keep within bounds, speak within probability, and we will believe you; but do not shock our reason. We will admit that we *ought* to be religious, and that, when we come to die, we shall be very glad to have led religious lives: but to tell us that it is a *pleasant* thing to be religious, this is too much: it is not true; we feel that it is not true; all the world knows and feels it is not true; religion is something unpleasant, gloomy, sad, and troublesome. It imposes a number of restraints on us; it keeps us from doing what we would; it will not let us have our own way; it abridges our liberty; it interferes with our enjoyments; it has fewer, far fewer, joys at present than a worldly life, though it gains for us more joys hereafter." This is what men say, or would say, if they understood what they feel, and spoke their minds freely.

Alas! I cannot deny that this *is* true in the case of most men. Most men do not like the service of God, though it be perfect freedom; they like to follow their own ways, and they are only religious so far as their conscience obliges them; they are like Balaam, desirous of "the death of the righteous," not of his life. Indeed, this is the very thing I am lamenting and deploring. I lament, my brethren, that so many men, nay, I may say, that so many of you, do *not* like religious service. I do not deny it; but I lament it. I do not deny it: far from it. I know quite well how many there are who do not like coming to Church, and who make excuses for

keeping away at times when they might come. I know
how many there are who do not come to the Most Holy
Sacrament. I know that there are numbers who do not
say their prayers in private morning and evening. I
know how many there are who are ashamed to be
thought religious, who take God's name in vain, and
live like the world. Alas! this is the very thing I
lament,—that God's service is not pleasant to you. It
is not pleasant to those who do not like it : true ; but it
is pleasant to those who *do*. Observe, this is what I
say ; not that it is pleasant to those who like it not, but
that it is pleasant to those who like it. Nay, what I
say is, that it is much *more* pleasant to those who like it,
than any thing of this world is pleasant to those who do
not like it. This is the point. I do not say that it is
pleasant to most men ; but I say that it is in itself the
most pleasant thing in the world. Nothing is so pleasant as God's service to those *to whom* it is pleasant.
The pleasures of sin are not to be compared in fulness
and intensity to the pleasures of holy living. The pleasures of holiness are far more pleasant to the holy, than
the pleasures of sin to the sinner. O that I could get
you to believe this! O that you had a heart to feel it
and know it! O that you had a heart to taste God's
pleasures and to make proof of them ; to taste and see
how gracious the Lord is!

None can know, however, the joys of being holy and
pure but the holy. If an Angel were to come down

from heaven, even he could not explain them to you ; nor could he in turn understand what the pleasures of sin are.   Do you think that an Angel could be made to understand what are the pleasures of sin ?   I trow not. You might as well attempt to persuade him that there was pleasure in feasting on dust and ashes.   There are brute animals who wallow in the mire and eat corruption.   This seems strange to us : much stranger to an Angel is it how any one can take pleasure in any thing so filthy, so odious, so loathsome as sin.   Many men, as I have been saying, wonder what possible pleasure there can be in any thing so melancholy as religion.   Well : be sure of this,—it is *more* wonderful to an Angel, what possible pleasure there can be in sinning.   It is *more* wonderful, I say.   He would turn away with horror and disgust, both because sin is so base a thing in itself, and because it is so hateful in God's sight.

. Let no persons then be surprised that religious obedience should really be so pleasant in itself, when it seems to them so distasteful.   Let them not be surprised that *what* the pleasure is cannot be explained to *them.* It is a secret till they try to be religious.   Men know what sin is, by experience.   They do not know what holiness is ; and they cannot obtain the knowledge of its secret pleasure, till they join themselves truly and heartily to Christ, and devote themselves to His service,—till they "taste," and thereby try.   This pleasure is as hidden from them, as the pleasures of sin are hidden from the Angels. The Angels have never eaten the forbidden fruit, and their eyes are not open to know good and evil. And we *have* eaten the forbidden fruit, —at least Adam did, and we are his descendants,—and our eyes *are* open to know evil. And, alas! on the other hand, they have become blinded to good; they require opening to see, to know, to understand good. And till our eyes *are* opened spiritually, we *shall* ever think religion distasteful and unpleasant, and shall wonder how any one can like it. Such is our miserable state,—we are blind to the highest and truest glories, and dead to the most lively and wonderful of all pleasures;—and no one can describe them to us. None other than God the Holy Spirit can help us in this matter, by enlightening and changing our hearts. So it is; and yet I will say one thing, by way of suggesting to you how great and piercing the joys of religion are. Think of this. Is there any one who does not know how very painful the feeling of a bad conscience is? Do not you recollect, my Brethren, some time or other, having done something you knew to be wrong? and do you not remember afterwards what a piercing bitter feeling came on you? Is not the feeling of a bad conscience different from any other feeling, and more distressing than any other, till we have accustomed ourselves to it? Persons do accustom themselves and lose this feeling; but till we blunt our conscience, it is very painful. And why? It is the feeling of God's displeasure, and therefore it is so painful. Consider then : if God's displeasure is so distressing to us, must not God's approval and favour be just the reverse ; like life from the dead, most exceedingly joyful and trans-porting ? And this is what it is to be holy and religious. It is to have God's favour.   And, as it is a great misery. to be under God's wrath, so it is a great and wonderful joy to be in God's favour ; and those who know what a misery the former is, may fancy, though they do not know, how high a blessing the latter is.   From what you know, then, judge of what you do not know.   From the miseries of guilt, which, alas ! you have experienced, conjecture the blessedness of holiness and purity which you have not experienced.   From the pain of a bad con-science, believe in the unspeakable joy and gladness of a good conscience.

I have been addressing those who do not know what religious peace and Divine pleasures are ; but there are those present, I hope, who in a measure are not strangers to them.   I know that none of us gain all the pleasure from God's service which it might afford us ; still some of us, I hope, gain some pleasure.   I hope there are some of those who hear me, who take a pleasure in coming to Church, in saying their prayers, in thinking. of God, in singing Psalms, in blessing Him for the mercies of the Gospel, and in celebrating Christ's death and resurrection, as at this season of the year[1].   These

---

[1] Easter.

persons have "tasted" and tried. I trust they find the taste so heavenly, that *they* will not need any proof that religion is a pleasant thing; nay, more pleasant than any thing else, worth the following above all other things, and unpleasant only to those who are not religious.

Let such persons then think of this, that if a religious life is pleasant here, in spite of the old Adam interrupting the pleasure and defiling them, what a glorious day it will be, if it is granted to us hereafter to enter into the Kingdom of Heaven! None of us, even the holiest, can guess *how* happy we shall be; for St. John says, "We know not what we shall be[1];" and St. Paul, "Now we see in a glass darkly, but then face to face." Yet in proportion to our present holiness and virtue, we have some faint ideas of what will then be our blessedness. And in Scripture various descriptions of heaven are given us, in order to arrest, encourage, and humble us. We are told that the Angels of God are very bright, and clad in white robes. The Saints and Martyrs too are clad in white robes, with palms in their hands; and they sing praises unto Him that sitteth upon the Throne, and to the Lamb. When our Lord was transfigured, He showed us what Heaven is. His raiment became white as snow, white and glistening. Again, at one time He appeared to St. John, and then, "His head and His hairs were white like wool, as white as snow;

[1] 1 John iii. 2.

and His eyes were as a flame of fire; and His feet like
unto fine brass, as if they burned in a furnace; and His
countenance was as the sun shineth in his strength[1]."
And what Christ is, such do His Saints become hereafter.   Here below they are clad in a garment of sinful
flesh; but when the end comes, and they rise from the
grave, they shall inherit glory, and shall be ever young
and ever shining.   In that day, all men will see and be
convinced, even bad men, that God's servants are really
happy, and only they.   In that day, even lost souls,
though they will not be able to understand the blessedness of religion, will have no doubt at all of what they
now doubt, or pretend to doubt, that religion *is* blessed.
They laugh at religion, think strictness to be narrow-
ness of mind, and regularity to be dulness; and give
bad names to religious men.   They will not be able to
do so then.   They think themselves the great men of
the earth now, and look down upon the religious; but
then, who would not have been a religious man, to have
so great a reward? who will then have any heart to
speak against religion, even though he has not "a heart
to fear God and keep all His commandments always?"
In that day, they will look upon the righteous man, and
"be amazed at the strangeness of his salvation, so far
beyond all that they looked for.   And they, repenting
and groaning for anguish of spirit, shall say within
themselves, This was he, whom we had sometimes in

[1] Rev. i. 14—16.

derision, and a proverb of reproach. We fools accounted his life madness, and his end to be without honour; how is he numbered among the children of God, and his lot is among the saints[1]!"

Think of all this, my Brethren, and rouse yourselves, and run forward with a good courage on your way towards heaven. Be not weary in well-doing, for in due season we shall reap, if we faint not. Strive to enter in at the strait gate. Strive to get holier and holier every day, that you may be worthy to stand before the Son of Man. Pray God to teach you His will, and to lead you forth in the right way, because of your enemies. Submit yourselves to His guidance, and you will have comfort given you, according to your day, and peace at the last.

[1] Wisd. v. 2—5.

SERMON XV.

MENTAL PRAYER.

1 Thess. v. 17.

"Pray without ceasing."

THERE are two modes of praying mentioned in Scripture; the one is prayer at set times and places, and in set forms; the other is what the text speaks of,—continual or habitual prayer. The former of these is what is commonly called prayer, whether it be public or private. The other kind of praying may also be called holding communion with God, or living in God's sight, and this may be done all through the day, wherever we are, and is commanded us as the duty, or rather the characteristic, of those who are really servants and friends of Jesus Christ.

These two kinds of praying are also natural duties. I mean, we should in a way be bound to attend to them, even if we were born in a heathen country and had never heard of the Bible. For our conscience and reason would lead us to practise them, if we did but attend to these divinely-given informants. I shall here confine myself to the consideration of the latter of the two, habitual or inward prayer, which is enjoined in the text, with the view of showing what it is, and how we are to practise it; and I shall speak of it, first, as a natural duty, and then as the characteristic of a Christian.

1. At first sight, it may be difficult to some persons to understand what is meant by praying always. Now consider it as a natural duty, that is, a duty taught us by natural reason and religious feeling, and you will soon see what it consists in.

What does nature teach us about ourselves, even before opening the Bible?—that we are creatures of the Great God, the Maker of heaven and earth; and that, as His creatures, we are bound to serve Him and give Him our hearts; in a word, to be religious beings. And next, what is religion but a habit? and what is a habit but a state of mind which is always upon us, as a sort of ordinary dress or inseparable garment of the soul? A man cannot really be religious one hour, and not religious the next. We might as well say he could be in a state of good health one hour, and in bad health the next. A man who is religious, is religious morning, noon, and night; his religion is a certain character, a mould in which his thoughts, words, and actions are cast, all forming parts of one and the same whole. He sees God in all things; every course of action he directs towards those spiritual objects which God has revealed to him; every occurrence of the day, every event, every person met with, all news which he hears, he measures by the standard of God's will. And a person who does this may be said almost literally to pray without ceasing; for, knowing himself to be in God's presence, he is continually led to address Him reverently, whom he sets always before him, in the inward language of prayer and praise, of humble confession and joyful trust.

All this, I say, any thoughtful man acknowledges from mere natural reason. To be religious is, in other words, to have the habit of prayer, or to pray always. This is what Scripture means by doing all things to God's glory; that is, so placing God's presence and will before us, and so consistently acting with a reference to Him, that all we do becomes one body and course of obedience, witnessing without ceasing to Him who made us, and whose servants we are; and in its separate parts promoting more or less directly His glory, according as each particular thing we happen to be doing admits more or less of a religious character. Thus religious obedience is, as it were, a spirit dwelling in us, extending its influence to every motion of the soul; and just as healthy men and strong men show their health and strength in all they do (not indeed equally in all things, but in some things more than in others, because all actions do not require or betoken the presence of that health and strength, and yet even in their step, and their voice, and their gestures, and their countenance, showing in due measure their vigour of body), so they who have the true health and strength of the soul, a clear, sober, and deep faith in Him in whom they have their being, will in all they do, nay (as St. Paul says), even whether they " eat or drink [1]," be living in God's sight, or, in the words of the same Apostle in the text, live in ceaseless prayer.

If it be said that no man on earth does thus continually and perfectly glorify and worship God, this we all know too well; this is only saying that none of us has reached perfection. We know, alas ! that in many things all of us offend. But I am speaking not of what we *do*, but of what we *ought to do*, and must aim at doing,—of *our duty ;* and, for the sake of impressing our duty on our hearts, it is of use to draw the picture of a man perfectly obedient, as a pattern for us to aim at. In proportion as we grow in grace and in the knowledge of our Saviour, so shall we approximate to Him in obedience, who is our great example, and who alone of all the sons of Adam lived in the perfection of unceasing prayer.

Thus the meaning and reasonableness of the command in the text is shown by considering it as a natural duty, religion being no accident which comes and goes by fits and starts, but a certain spirit or life.

2. Now, secondly, I will state all this in the language of Scripture; that is, I will confirm this view of our

[1] 1 Cor. x. 31.

duty, which natural reason might suggest, by that other and far clearer voice of God, His inspired word.

How is religious obedience described in Scripture? Surely as a certain kind of life. We know what life of the body is; it is a state of the body: the pulse beats; all things are in motion. The hidden principle of life, though we know not how or what it is, is seen in these outward signs of it. And so of the life of the soul. The soul, indeed, was not possessed of this life of God when first born into the world. We are born with dead souls; that is, dead as regards religious obedience. If left to ourselves we should grow up haters of God, and tend nearer and nearer, the longer we had existence, to utter spiritual death, that inward fire of hell torments, maturing in evil through a long eternity. Such is the course we are beginning to run when born into the world; and were it not for the gospel promise, what a miserable event would the birth of children be! Who could take pleasure at the sight of such poor beings, unconscious as yet of their wretchedness, but containing in their hearts that fearful root of sin which is sure in the event of reigning and triumphing unto everlasting woe? But God has given us all, even the little children, a good promise through Christ; and our prospects are changed. And He has given not only a promise of future happiness, but through His Holy Spirit He implants here and at once a new principle within us, a new spiritual life, a life of the soul, as it is called. St. Paul tells us, that "God hath quickened us," made us *live*, "together with Christ, . . . and hath raised us up together" from the death of sin, "and made us sit together in heavenly places in Christ Jesus[1]." Now how God quickens our souls we do not know; as little as how He quickens our bodies. Our spiritual "life" (as St. Paul says) "is *hid* with Christ in God[2]." But as our bodily life discovers itself by its activity, so is the presence of the Holy Spirit in us discovered by a spiritual activity; and this activity is the spirit of continual prayer. Prayer is to spiritual life what the beating of the pulse and the drawing of the breath are to the life of the body. It would be as absurd to suppose that life could last when the body was cold and motionless and senseless, as to call a soul alive which does not pray. The state or habit of spiritual life exerts itself, consists, in the continual activity of prayer.

Do you ask, where does Scripture say this? Where? In all it tells us of the connexion between the new birth and faith; for what is prayer but the expression, the voice, of faith? For instance, St. Paul says to the Galatians, "The *life* which I now live in the flesh" (i. e. the new and spiritual life), "I live by the *faith* of the Son of God, who loved me[3]." For what, I say, is faith, but the looking to God and thinking of Him continually, holding habitual fellowship with Him, that

[1] Eph. ii. 5, 6.   [2] Col. iii. 3.   [3] Gal. ii. 20.

is, speaking to Him in our hearts all through the day, praying without ceasing? Afterwards, in the same Epistle, he tells us first that nothing avails but faith working by love; but soon after, he calls this same availing principle a new creature : so that the new birth and a living faith are inseparable. Never, indeed, must it be supposed, as we are indolently apt to suppose, that the gift of grace which we receive at baptism is a mere outward privilege, a mere outward pardon, in which the heart is not concerned; or as if it were some mere mark put on the soul, distinguishing it indeed from souls unregenerate, as if by a colour or seal, but not connected with the thoughts, mind, and heart of a Christian. This would be a gross and false view of the nature of God's mercy given us in Christ. For the new birth of the Holy Spirit sets the soul in motion in a heavenly way : it gives us good thoughts and desires, enlightens and purifies us, and prompts us to seek God. In a word (as I have said), it gives a spiritual *life;* it opens the eyes of our mind, so that we begin to see God in all things by faith, and hold continual intercourse with Him by prayer; and if we cherish these gracious influences, we shall become holier and wiser and more heavenly, year by year, our hearts being ever in a course of change from darkness to light, from the ways and works of Satan to the perfection of Divine obedience.

These considerations may serve to impress upon our

minds the meaning of the precept in the text, and others like it which are found in St. Paul's Epistles. For instance, he enjoins the Ephesians to "pray always with all prayer and supplication in the Spirit." To the Philippians he says, "Be careful for nothing; but in every thing by prayer and supplication let your requests be made known unto God[1]." To the Colossians, "Continue in prayer, and watch in the same with thanksgiving." To the Romans, "Continue instant in prayer[2]."

Thus the true Christian pierces through the veil of this world and sees the next. He holds intercourse with it; he addresses God, as a child might address his parent, with as clear a view of Him, and with as unmixed a confidence in Him; with deep reverence indeed, and godly fear and awe, but still with certainty and exactness : as St. Paul says, "I know whom I have believed[3]," with the prospect of judgment to come to sober him, and the assurance of present grace to cheer him.

If what I have said is true, surely it is well worth thinking about. Most men indeed, I fear, neither pray at fixed times, nor do they cultivate an habitual communion with Almighty God. Indeed, it is too plain how most men pray. They pray now and then, when they feel particular need of God's assistance; when they

---

[1] Eph. vi. 18.   Phil. iv. 6.   [2] Col. iv. 2.   Rom. xii. 12.
[3] 2 Tim. i. 12.

are in trouble or in apprehension of danger; or when their feelings are unusually excited. They do not know what it is either to be habitually religious, or to devote a certain number of minutes at fixed times to the thought of God. Nay, the very best Christian, how lamentably deficient is he in the spirit of prayer! Let any man compare in his mind how many times he has prayed when in trouble, with how seldom he has returned thanks when his prayers have been granted; or the earnestness with which he prays against expected suffering, with the languor and unconcern of his thanksgivings afterwards, and he will soon see how little he has of the real habit of prayer, and how much his religion depends on accidental excitement, which is no test of a religious heart. Or supposing he has to repeat the same prayer for a month or two, the cause of using it continuing, let him compare the earnestness with which he first said it, and tried to enter into it, with the coldness with which he at length uses it. Why is this, except that his perception of the unseen world is not the true view which faith gives (else it would last as that world itself lasts), but a mere dream, which endures for a night, and is succeeded by a hard worldly joy in the morning? Is God habitually in our thoughts? Do we think of Him, and of His Son our Saviour, through the day? When we eat and drink, do we thank Him, not as a mere matter of form, but in spirit? When we do things in themselves right, do we lift up our minds to Him, and desire to promote His glory? When we are in the exercise of our callings, do we still think of Him, acting ever conscientiously, desiring to know His will more exactly than we do at present, and aiming at fulfilling it more completely and abundantly? Do we wait on His grace to enlighten, renew, strengthen us?

I do not ask whether we use many words about religion. There is no need to do this: nay, we should avoid a boastful display of our better feelings and practices, silently serving God without human praise, and hiding our conscientiousness except when it would dishonour God to do so. There are times, indeed, when, in the presence of a holy man, to confess is a benefit, and there are times when, in the presence of worldly men, to confess becomes a duty; but these seasons, whether of privilege or of duty, are comparatively rare. But we are always with ourselves and our God; and that silent inward confession in His presence may be sustained and continual, and will end in durable fruit.

But if those persons come short of their duty who make religion a matter of impulse and mere feeling, what shall be said to those who have no feeling or thought of religion at all? What shall be said of the multitude of young people who ridicule seriousness, and deliberately give themselves up to vain thoughts? Alas! my brethren, you do not even observe or recognize the foolish empty thoughts which pass through your

minds; you are not distressed even at those of them you
recollect; but what will you say at the last day, when,
instead of the true and holy visions in which consists
Divine communion, you find recorded against you in
God's book an innumerable multitude of the idlest,
silliest imaginings, nay, of the wickedest, which ever
disgraced an immortal being? What will you say,
when heaven and hell are before you, and the books are
opened, and therein you find the sum total of your
youthful desires and dreams, your passionate wishes for
things of this world, your low-minded, grovelling tastes,
your secret contempt and aversion for serious subjects
and persons, your efforts to attract the looks of sinners
and to please those who displease God; your hankerings
after worldly gaieties and luxuries, your admiration of
the rich or titled, your indulgence of impure thoughts,
your self-conceit and pitiful vanity? Ah, I may seem
to you to use harsh words; but be sure I do not use
terms near so severe as you will use against yourselves
in that day. Then those men, whom you now think
gloomy and over-strict, will seem to you truly wise;
and the advice to pray without ceasing, which once you
laughed at as fit only for the dull, the formal, the sour,
the poor-spirited, or the aged, will be approved by your
own experience, as it is even now by your reason and
conscience. Oh, that you could be brought to give one
serious hour to religion, in anticipation of that long
eternity where you *must* be serious! True, you may

laugh now, but there is no vain merriment on the other
side of the grave. The devils, though they repent not,
tremble. *You* will be among those unwilling serious
ones then, if you are mad enough to be gay and careless
now; if you are mad enough to laugh, jest, and scoff
your poor moment now on earth, which is short enough
to prepare for eternity in, without your making it shorter
by wasting your youth in sin. Could you but see who
it is that suggests to you all your lighter thoughts,
which you put instead of Divine communion, the shock
would make you serious, even if it did not make you
religious. Could you see, what God sees, those snares
and pitfalls which the devil is placing about your path;
could you see that all your idle thoughts which you
cherish, which seem so bright and pleasant, so much
pleasanter than religious thoughts, are inspired by that
Ancient Seducer of Mankind, the Author of Evil, who
stands at your side while you deride religion, serious
indeed himself while he makes you laugh, not able to
laugh at his own jests, while he carries you dancing
forward to perdition,—doubtless you would tremble,
even as he does while he tempts you. But this you
cannot possibly see, you cannot break your delusion,
except by first taking God's word in this matter on
trust. You cannot see the unseen world at once. They
who ever speak with God in their hearts, are in turn
taught by Him in all knowledge; but they who refuse
to act upon the light, which God gave them by nature,

at length come to lose it altogether, and are given up to a reprobate mind.

May God save us all from such wilful sin, old as well as young, and enlighten us one and all in His saving knowledge, and give us the will and the power to serve Him!

SERMON XVI.

INFANT BAPTISM.

JOHN iii. 5.

"Except a man be born of water and of the Spirit, he cannot enter into the Kingdom of God."

NONE can be saved, unless the blood of Christ, the Immaculate Lamb of God, be imputed to him; and it is His gracious will that it should be imputed to us, one by one, by means of outward and visible signs, or what are called Sacraments. These visible rites represent to us the heavenly truth, and convey what they represent. The baptismal washing betokens the cleansing of the soul from sin; the elements of bread and wine are figures of what is present but not seen, " the body and blood of Christ, which are verily and indeed taken and received by the faithful in the Lord's Supper." So far the two Sacraments agree; yet there is this important difference in their use,—that Baptism is but *once* administered, but the Lord's Supper is to be received *continually.* Our Lord Christ told the Apostles to baptize *at the time* that they made men His disciples.

Baptism *admitted* them to His favour once for all; but the Lord's Supper *keeps* us and secures us in His favour day by day. He said, "This do, *as often as* ye drink it, in *remembrance* of Me."

Here, then, a question at once arises, which it is important to consider :—*At what time* in our life are we to be baptized, or made disciples of Christ? The first Christians of course were baptized when they were come to a full age, because then the Gospel was for the first time preached to them; they had no means of being baptized when young. But the case is different with those who are born of Christian parents; so the question now is, at what age are the sons of Christians to be baptized?

Now, for fifteen hundred years there was no dispute or difficulty in answering this question all over the Christian world; none who acknowledged the duty of baptizing at all, but administered the rite to infants, as we do at present. But about three hundred years ago strange opinions were set afloat, and sects arose, doing every thing which had not been done before, and undoing every thing that had been done before, and all this (as they professed) on the principle that it was every one's duty to judge and act for himself; and among these new sects there was one which maintained that Infant Baptism was a mistake, and that, mainly upon this short argument,—that it was nowhere commanded in Scripture.

Let us, then, consider this subject: and first, it is but fair and right to acknowledge at once that Scripture does *not* bid us baptize children. This, however, is no very serious admission; for Scripture does not name *any* time at all for Baptism; yet it orders us to be baptized at some age or other. It is plain, then, whatever age we fix upon, we shall be going beyond the letter of Scripture. This may or may not be a difficulty, but it cannot be avoided: it is not a difficulty of *our* making. God has so willed it. He has kept silence, and doubtless with good reason; and surely we must try to do our part and to find out what He would have us do, according to the light, be it greater or less, which He has vouchsafed to us.

Is it any new thing that it should take time and thought to find out accurately what our duty is? Is it a new thing that the full and perfect truth should not lie on the very surface of things, in the bare letter of Scripture? Far from it. Those who *strive* to enter into life, these alone find the strait gate which leads thereto. It is no proof even that it is a matter of indifference what age is proper for Baptism, that Scripture is not clear about it, but hides its real meaning; not commanding but hinting what we should do. For consider how many things in this life are difficult to attain, yet, far from being matters of indifference, are necessary for our comfort or even well-being. Nay, it often happens that the more valuable any gift is, the more difficult it is to gain it. Take, for instance, the art of medicine. Is there an art more important for our life and comfort? Yet how difficult and uncertain is the science of it! what time it takes to be well versed and practised in it! What would be thought of a person who considered that it mattered little whether a sick man took this course or that, on the ground that men were not physicians by nature, and that if the Creator had meant medicine to be for our good, He would have told us at once, and every one of us, the science and the practice of it? In the same way it does not at all follow, even if it *were* difficult to find out at what age Baptism should be administered, that therefore one time is as good as another. Difficulty is the very attendant upon great blessings, not on things indifferent.

But a man may say that Scripture is given us for the very purpose of making the knowledge of our duty easy to us;—what is meant by a revelation, if it does not reveal?—and that we have no revelation to tell us what medicines are good or bad for the body, but that a revelation *has* been made in order to tell us what is good or bad for the soul:—if, then, a thing *were* important for our soul's benefit, Scripture would have plainly declared it. I answer, who told us all this? Doubtless, Scripture *was* given to make our duty *easier than before;* but how do we know that it was intended to take away *all* difficulty of every kind? So says not Christ, when He bids us seek and strive and so find; to knock, to watch, and to pray. No; Scripture has not undertaken to *tell* us every thing, but merely to give us the means of *finding* every thing; and thus much we can conclude on the subject before us, that if it is important, there are *means* of determining it; but we cannot infer, either that it must actually be *commanded* in the letter of Scripture, or that it can be found out by every individual *for and by himself*.

But it may be said, Scripture says that the times of the Gospel shall be times of great light: " All thy children shall be taught of the Lord, and great shall be the peace of thy children [1]." This is true : but whose children? The Church's. Surely it *is* a time of light, if we come to the Church for information; for she has ever spoken most clearly on the subject. She has ever baptized infants and enjoined the practice; she has ever answered to the prophecy as being "a word behind us, saying, This is the way; walk ye in it." Her teachers surely (according to the prophecy) have never been removed into a corner. But if we will not accept this supernatural mercy, then I say it is not unnatural that we should find ourselves in the same kind of doubt in which we commonly are involved in matters of this world. God has promised us light and knowledge in the Gospel, but in His way, not in *our* way.

But after all, in the present instance, surely there is no great difficulty in finding out what God would have

[1] Isa. liv. 13.

us to do, though He has not told us in Scripture in the plainest way. I say it is not difficult to see, as the Church has ever been led to see, that God would have us baptize young children, and that to delay Baptism is to delay a great benefit, and is hazarding a child's salvation. There is no difficulty, if men are not resolved to make one.

1. Let us consider, first, what is Baptism? It is a means and pledge of God's mercy, pardon, acceptance of us for Christ's sake; it gives us grace to change our natures. Now, surely infants, as being born in sin, have most abundant *need* of God's mercy and grace: this cannot be doubted. Even at first sight, then, it appears *desirable* (to say the least) that they should be baptized. Baptism is just suited to their need: it contains a promise of the very blessings which they want, and which without God's free bounty they cannot have. If, indeed, Baptism were merely or principally *our* act, then perhaps the case would be altered. But it is not an act of ours so much as of God's; a pledge from Him. And, I repeat, infants, as being by nature under God's wrath, having no elements of spiritual life in them, being corrupt and sinful, are surely, in a singular manner, objects of Baptism as far as the question of desirableness is concerned.

Let us refer to our Saviour's words to Nicodemus in the text. Our Lord tells him none can enter into the kingdom of God who is not born of water and the Spirit.

And why? *Because* (He goes on to say) "that which is born of the flesh is flesh [1]." We need a new birth, because our first birth is a birth unto sin. Who does not see that this reason is equally cogent for *infant* Baptism as for Baptism at all? Baptism by water and the Spirit is necessary for salvation (He says), *because* man's *nature* is corrupt; therefore infants must need this regeneration too. If, indeed, sin were not planted deep in man's very heart,—if it were merely an accidental evil into which some fell while others escaped it,—nay, even if, though (as a fact) all men actually fall into sin, yet this general depravity arose merely from bad example, not from natural bias, then indeed Baptism of water and the Spirit would not be necessary except for those who, having come to years of understanding, had actual sin to answer for: but if, as our Saviour implies, even a child's heart, before he begins to think and act, is under Divine wrath, and contains the sure and miserable promise of future sin as the child grows up, can we do otherwise than thankfully accept the pledge and means which He has given us of a new birth unto holiness; and since, by not telling us the time for Baptism, He has in a way left it to ourselves to decide upon it, shall we not apply the medicine given us when we are sure of the disease? "Can any man *forbid* water," to use St. Peter's words under different circumstances, "that" children "should not be baptized?" The burden of

[1] John iii. 6.

proof, as it is called, is with those who withhold the Sacrament.

Will it be said that infants are not properly *qualified* for Baptism? How is this an objection? Consider the text.—"Except one be born of water and the Spirit," says our Lord, "he cannot enter into the kingdom of God." There is nothing said about qualifications or conditions here which might exclude infants from Baptism,—nothing about the necessity of previous faith, or previous good works, in order to fit us for the mercy of God. Nor indeed could any thing be said. Christ knew that, without His grace, man's nature could not bear any good fruit, for from above is every good gift. Far from it. Any such notion of man's unassisted strength is wholly detestable, contrary to the very first principles of all true religion, whether Jewish, Christian, or even Pagan. We are miserably fallen creatures, we are by nature corrupt,—we dare not talk even of children being naturally pleasing in God's sight. And if we wait till children are in a condition to bring something to God, in payment (so to say) of His mercy to them, till they have faith and repentance, they never will be baptized; for they will never attain to that condition. To defer Baptism till persons actually have repentance and faith, is refusing to give medicine till a patient begins to get well. It would be hard indeed, if Satan be allowed to have access to the soul from infancy, as soon as it begins to think, and we refuse to do what we can, or

what promises well, towards gaining for it the protection of God against the Tempter.

On this first view of the case then, from the original
corruption of our nature, from the need which all men
are under from their birth of pardon and help from God,
from Baptism being a promise of mercy just suited to
our need, and from the impossibility of any one (let him
be allowed to live unbaptized ever so long) bringing
any self-provided recommendation of himself to God's
favour; on all these accounts, I say, since God has given
us no particular directions in the matter, but has left it
to ourselves, it seems, on the first view of the case, most
fitting and right to give children the privilege of Baptism.

2. But, in fact, we are not, strictly speaking, left
without positive encouragement to bring infants near to
Him. We are not merely left to infer generally the
propriety of Infant Baptism; Christ has shown us His
willingness to receive children. Some men have said
(indeed most of us perhaps in seasons of unbelief have
been tempted in our hearts to ask), "What good can
Baptism do senseless children? you might as well baptize things without life; they sleep or even struggle
during the ceremony, and interrupt it; it is a mere
superstition." This, my brethren, is the language of
the world, whoever uses it. It is putting sight against
faith. If we are assured that Baptism has been blessed
by Christ, as the rite of admittance into His Church, we

[VII]   Q

have nothing to do with those outward appearances, which, though they might prove something perhaps, had He not spoken, now that He has spoken lose all force. To such objections, I would reply by citing our Saviour's "own word and deed." We find that infants *were* brought to Christ; and His disciples seem to have doubted, in the same spirit of unbelief, what *could* be the good of bringing helpless and senseless children to the Saviour of men. They doubtless thought that His time would be better employed in teaching *them*, than in attending to children; that it was interfering with His usefulness. "But when Jesus saw it, He was much displeased [1]." These are remarkable words: "much displeased,"—that is, He was uneasy, indignant, angry (as the Greek word may be more literally translated); and we are told, "He took them up in His arms, put His hands upon them, and *blessed them.*" Christ, then, *can* bless infants, in spite of their being to all appearance as yet incapable of thought or feeling. He can, and did, bless them; and, in the very sense in which they then were blessed, we believe they are capable of a blessing in Baptism.

3. And we may add this consideration. It is certain that children ought to be instructed in religious truth, as they can bear it, from the very first dawn of reason; clearly, they are not to be left without a Christian training till they arrive at years of maturity. Now, let

---

[1] Mark x. 14.

it be observed, Christ seems distinctly to connect teaching with Baptism, as if He intended to convey through it a blessing upon teaching,—" Go ye and teach all the nations, baptizing them." If children, then, are to be considered as under teaching, as learners in the school of Christ, surely they should be admitted into that school by Baptism.

These are the reasons for Infant Baptism which strike the mind, even on the first consideration of the subject; and in the absence of express information from Scripture, they are (as far as they go) satisfactory. At *what age* should we be baptized? I answer, in childhood; because all children *require* Divine pardon and grace (as our Saviour Himself implies), all are *capable* of His blessing (as His action shows), all are *invited* to His blessing, and Baptism is a pledge from Him of His favour, as His Apostles frequently declare. Since infants are to be brought to Christ, we must have invented a rite, if Baptism did not answer the purpose of a dedication. Again, I say, in childhood; because all children need Christian instruction, and Baptism is a badge and mark of a scholar in Christ's school. And moreover, I will add, because St. Paul speaks of the children of Christian parents as being " holy," in a favoured state, a state of unmerited blessing; and because he seems to have baptized at once whole families, where the head of the family was converted to the faith of the Gospel[1].

[1] 1 Cor. vii. 14.   Acts xvi. 15. 33.

Q 2

To conclude.   Let me beg of all who hear me, and who wish to serve God, to remember, in their ordinary prayers, their habitual thoughts, the daily business of life, that they were once baptized.   If Baptism be merely a ceremony, to be observed indeed, but then at once forgotten,—a decent form, which it would neither be creditable, nor for temporal reasons expedient to neglect, —it is most surely no subject for a Christian minister to speak of; Christ's religion has no fellowship with bare forms, and nowhere encourages mere outward observances.   If, indeed, there be any who degrade Baptism into a mere ceremony, which has in it no spiritual promise, let such men look to it for themselves, and defend their practice of baptizing infants as they can. But for me, my brethren, I would put it before you as a true and plain pledge, without reserve, of God's grace given to the souls of those who receive it; not a mere form, but a real means and instrument of blessing verily and indeed received; and, as being such, I warn you to remember what a talent has been committed to you. There are very many persons who do not think of Baptism in this religious point of view; who are in no sense in the habit of blessing God for it, and praying Him for His further grace to profit by the privileges given them in it; who, when even they pray for grace, do not ground their hope of being heard and answered, on the promise of blessing in Baptism made to them; above all, who do not fear to sin after Baptism.   This is of course an omission; in many cases it is a *sin*. Let us set ourselves right in this respect. Nothing will remind us more forcibly both of our advantages and of our duties; for from the very nature of our minds outward signs are especially calculated (if rightly used) to strike, to affect, to subdue, to change them.

Blessed is he who makes the most of the privileges given him, who takes them for a light to his feet and a lanthorn to his path. We have had the Sign of the Cross set on us in infancy,—shall we ever forget it? It is our profession. We had the water poured on us,—it was like the blood on the door-posts, when the destroying Angel passed over. Let us fear to sin after grace given, lest a worse thing come upon us. Let us aim at learning these two great truths:—that we can do nothing good without God's grace, yet that we can sin against that grace; and thus that the great gift may be made the cause, on the one hand, of our gaining eternal life, and the occasion to us, on the other, of eternal misery.

SERMON XVII.

THE UNITY OF THE CHURCH.

MATT. xvi. 18.

" And I say also unto thee, That thou art Peter, and upon this rock I will build My Church; and the gates of hell shall not prevail against it."

TOO many persons at this day,—in spite of what they see before them, in spite of what they read in history,—too many persons forget, or deny, or do not know, that Christ has set up a kingdom in the world. In spite of the prophecies, in spite of the Gospels and Epistles, in spite of their eyes and their ears,—whether it be their sin or their misfortune, so it is,—they do not obey Him in that way in which it is His will that He should be obeyed. They do not obey Him in His Kingdom; they think to be His people, without being His subjects. They determine to serve Him in their own way; and though He has formed His chosen into one body, they think to separate from that body, yet to remain in the number of the chosen.

Far different is the doctrine suggested to us by the

text. In St. Peter, who is there made the rock on which the Church is founded, we see, as in a type, its unity, stability, and permanence. It is set up in one name, not in many, to show that it is one; and that name is Peter, to show that it will last, or, as the Divine Speaker proceeds, that "the gates of hell shall not prevail against it." In like manner, St. Paul calls it "the pillar and ground of the truth [1]."

This is a subject especially brought before us at this time of year [2], and it may be well now to enlarge upon it.

Now that all Christians are, in some sense or other, one, in our Lord's eyes, is plain, from various parts of the New Testament. In His mediatorial prayer for them to the Almighty Father, before His passion, He expressed His purpose that they should be *one*. St. Paul, in like manner, writing to the Corinthians, says, "As the body is one, and hath many members, and all the members of that one body, being many, are one body, *so also* is Christ. . . . . . Now ye are *the Body* of Christ, and members in particular." To the Ephesians, he says, "There is *one Body*, and one Spirit, even as ye are called in one hope of your calling: one Lord, one faith, one baptism, one God and Father of all [3]."

And, further, it is to this one Body, regarded as one,

[1] 1 Tim. iii. 15.   [2] Easter and Whitsuntide.
[3] John xvii. 23.   1 Cor. xii. 12.   Eph. iv. 4—6.

that the special privileges of the Gospel are given.   It
is not that this man receives the blessing, and that man,
but one and all, the whole body, as one man, one new
spiritual man, with one accord, seeks and gains it.   The
Holy Church throughout the world, "the Bride, the
Lamb's wife," is one, not many, and the elect souls are
all elected in her, not in isolation.   For instance; " He
is our peace who hath made both [Jews and Gentiles]
one, . . . to make in Himself of twain *one new man.*"
In the same Epistle, it is said, that all nations are
"*fellow*-heirs, and of *the same body*, and *fellow-partakers*
of His promise in Christ;" and that we must " one and
all come," or converge, " in the unity of the faith and
of the knowledge of the Son of God, unto a perfect
man, unto the measure of the stature of the fulness of
Christ;" that as " the husband is the head of the wife,"
so " Christ is the Head of the Church," having "loved
it and given Himself for it, that He might sanctify and
cleanse it with the washing of water by the Word[1]."
These are a few out of many passages which connect
Gospel privileges with the circumstance or condition of
unity in those who receive them; the image of Christ
and token of their acceptance being stamped upon them
then, at that moment, when they are considered as *one ;*
so that henceforth the whole multitude, no longer
viewed as mere individual men, become portions or
members of the indivisible Body of Christ Mystical, so

[1] Eph. ii. 14; iii. 6; iv. 13; v. 23—26.

knit together in Him by Divine Grace, that all have what He has, and each has what all have.

The same great truth is taught us in such texts as speak of all Christians forming one spiritual building, of which the Jewish Temple was the type. They are temples one by one, simply as being portions of that one Temple which is the Church. " Ye are *built up*," says St. Peter, " a spiritual house, a holy priesthood, to offer spiritual sacrifices acceptable to God by Jesus Christ." Hence the word " edification," which properly means this building up of all Christians in one, has come to stand for individual improvement; for it is by being incorporated into the one Body, that we have the promise of life ; by becoming members of Christ, we have the gift of His Spirit.

Further, that unity is the condition of our receiving the privileges of the Gospel is confirmed by the mode in which the Prophets describe the Christian Church ; that is, instead of addressing individuals as independent and separate from each other, they view the whole as of one body ; viz. that one elect, holy, and highly-favoured Mother, of which individuals are but the children favoured through her as a channel. " Lift up thine eyes, and behold," says the inspired announcement ; " all these gather themselves together, and come to thee." " O thou afflicted, tossed with tempest, and not comforted. behold, I will lay thy stones with fair colours, and lay thy foundations with sapphires. . . . . All thy children shall be taught of the Lord, and great shall be the peace of thy children."

But here it may be asked, How is this a doctrine to affect our practice ? That Christians may be considered in our minds as one, is evident ; it is evident, too, that they must be one in spirit ; and that hereafter they will be one blessed company in heaven ; but what follows now from believing that all saints are one in Christ ? *This* will be found to follow : that, as far as may be, Christians should live together in a visible society here on earth, not as a confused unconnected multitude, but united and organized one with another, by an established order, so as evidently to appear and to act as one. And this, you will at once see, *is* a doctrine nearly affecting our practice, yet neglected far and wide at this day.

Any complete and accurate proof indeed of this doctrine shall not here be attempted; nay, I shall not even bring together, as is often done [1], the more obvious texts on which it rests ; let it suffice, on this occasion, to make one or two general remarks bearing upon it, and strongly recommending it to us.

1. When, then, I am asked, why we Christians must unite into a visible body or society, I answer, first, that the very earnestness with which Scripture insists upon a spiritual unseen unity at present, and a future unity in heaven, of itself directs a pious mind to the imitation of

[1] Vide Tracts for the Times, No. 11.

that unity visible on earth; for why should it be so continually mentioned in Scripture, unless the thought of it were intended to sink deep into our minds, and direct our conduct here?

2. But again, our Saviour prays that we may be one in affection and in action; yet what possible way is there of many men acting *together,* except that of forming themselves into a visible body or society, regulated by certain laws and officers? and how can they act on a large scale, and consistently, unless it be a permanent body?

3. But, again, I might rest the necessity of Christian unity upon one single institution of our Lord's, the Sacrament of Baptism. Baptism is a visible rite confessedly; and St. Paul tells us that, by it, individuals are incorporated into an already existing body. He is speaking of the visible body of Christians, when he says, "By one Spirit are we all baptized *into one body*[1]." But if every one who wishes to become a Christian must come to an existing visible body for the gift, as these words imply, it is plain that no number of men can ever, consistently with Christ's intention, set up a Church for themselves. All must receive their Baptism from Christians already baptized, and they in their turn must have received the Sacrament from former Christians, themselves already incorporated in a body then previously existing. And thus we trace back a visible

[1] 1 Cor. xii. 13.

body or society even to the very time of the Apostles themselves; and it becomes plain that there can be no Christian in the whole world who has not received his title to the Christian privileges from the original apostolical society.   So that the very Sacrament of Baptism, as prescribed by our Lord and His Apostles, implies the existence of one visible association of Christians, and only one; and that permanent, carried on by the succession of Christians from the time of the Apostles to the very end of the world.

This is the *design* of Christ, I say, implied in the institution of the baptismal rite.   Whether He will be merciful, over and above His promise, to those who through ignorance do not comply with this design, or are in other respects irregular in their obedience, is a further question, foreign to our purpose.   Still it remains the revealed design of Christ to connect all His followers in one by a visible ordinance of incorporation. The Gospel faith has not been left to the world at large, recorded indeed in the Bible, but there left, like other important truths, to be taken up by men or rejected, as it may happen.   Truths, indeed, in science and the arts *have* been thus left to the chance adoption or neglect of mankind; they are no one's property; cast at random upon the waves of human opinion.   In any country soever, men may appropriate them at once, and form themselves at their will into a society for their extension.   But for the more momentous truths of revealed religion, the God, who wrought by human means in their first introduction, still preserves them by the same. Christ formed a body; He secured that body from dissolution by the bond of a Sacrament. He committed the privileges of His spiritual kingdom and the maintenance of His faith as a legacy to this baptized society; and into it, as a matter of historical fact, all the nations *have* flowed. Christianity has not been spread, as other systems, in an isolated manner, or by books; but from a centre, by regularly formed bodies, descendants of the three thousand, who, after St. Peter's preaching on the day of Pentecost, joined themselves to the Apostles' doctrine and fellowship.

And to this apostolical body we must still look for the elementary gift of grace. Grace will not baptize us while we sit at home, slighting the means which God has appointed; but we must "*come* unto Mount Sion, and unto the city of the living God, the heavenly Jerusalem, and to an innumerable company of angels, to the general assembly and Church of the first-born which are written in heaven, and to God the Judge of all, and to the spirits of just men made perfect, and to Jesus the mediator of the new covenant, and to the blood of sprinkling that speaketh better things than that of Abel."

4. And now I will mention one other guarantee, which is especially suggested by our Lord's words in the text, for the visible unity and permanence of His

Church; and that is the appointment of rulers and ministers, entrusted with the gifts of grace, and these in succession. The ministerial orders are the ties which bind together the whole body of Christians in one; they are its organs, and they are moreover its moving principle.

Such an institution necessarily implies a succession, unless the appointment was always to be miraculous; for if men cannot administer to themselves the rite of regeneration, it is surely as little or much less reasonable to suppose that they could become Bishops or Priests on their own ordination. And St. Paul expressly shows his solicitude to secure such a continuity of clergy for his brethren: "I left thee in Crete," he says to Titus, "that thou shouldest set in order the things that are wanting, and *ordain elders* in every city, as I had appointed thee [1]." And to Timothy: "The things that thou hast heard of me among many witnesses, the same *commit thou to faithful men,* who shall be able to teach others also [2]."

Now, we know that in civil matters nothing tends more powerfully to strengthen and perpetuate the body politic than hereditary rulers and nobles. The father's life, his principles and interests, are continued in the son; or rather, one life, one character, one idea, is carried on from age to age. Thus a dynasty or a nation is consolidated and secured; whereas where there is no

[1] Titus i. 5.   [2] 2 Tim. ii. 2.   Vide also 1 Tim. v. 22.

regular succession and inheritance of this kind, there is no safeguard of stability and tranquillity ; or rather, there is every risk of revolution. For what is to make a succeeding age think and act in the spirit of the foregoing, but that tradition of opinion and usage from mind to mind which a succession involves? In like manner the Christian ministry affects the unity, inward and without, of the Church to which it is attached. It is a continuous office, a standing ordinance ; not, indeed, transmitted from father to son, as under the Mosaic covenant, for the vessels of the Christian election need to be more special, as the treasure committed to them is more heavenly : but still the Apostles have not left it to the mere good pleasure and piety of the Christian body whether they will have a ministry or not. Each preceding generation of clergy have it in charge to ordain the next following to their sacred office. Consider what would be sure to happen, were there no such regular trans-mission of the Divine gift, but each congregation were left to choose and create for itself its own minister. This would follow, among other evil consequences, that what is every one's duty would prove, as the proverb runs, to be no one's. When their minister or teacher died or left them, there would be first a delay in choosing a fresh one, then a reluctance, then a forgetfulness. At last congregations would be left without teachers ; and the bond of union being gone, the Church would be broken up. If a ministry be a necessary part of the

Gospel Dispensation, so must also a ministerial succession be.   But the gift of grace has not thus dropped out of the hands of its All-merciful Giver.   He has committed to certain of His servants to provide for the continuance of its presence and its administration after their own time.   Each generation provides for the next; "the parents" lay up "for the children."   And we know as a fact, that to this day the ministers of the Church universal are descended from the very Apostles. Amid all the changes of this world, the Church built upon St. Peter and the rest has continued until now in the unbroken line of the ministry.   And to put other considerations out of sight, the mere fact in itself, that there has been this perpetual succession, this unforfeited inheritance, is sufficiently remarkable to attract our attention and excite our reverence.   It approves itself to us as providential, and enlivens our hope and trust, that an ordinance, thus graciously protected for so many hundred years, will continue unto the end, and that "the gates of hell shall not prevail against it."

I shall now bring these remarks to an end.   And in ending, let me remind you, my brethren, how nearly the whole doctrine of ecclesiastical order is connected with personal obedience to God's will.   Obedience to the rule of order is every where enjoined in Scripture; obedience to it is an act of faith.   Were there ten thousand objections to it, yet, supposing unity were clearly and expressly enjoined by Christ, faith would obey in spite of them. But in matter of fact there are no such objections, nor any difficulty of any moment in the way of observing it. What, then, is to be said to the very serious circumstance, that, in spite of the absence of such impediments, vast numbers of men conceive that they may dispense with it at their good pleasure. In all the controversies of fifteen hundred years, the duty of continuing in order and in quietness was professed on all sides, as one of the first principles of the Gospel of Christ. But now multitudes, both in and without the Church, have set it up on high as a great discovery, and glory in it as a great principle, that forms are worth nothing. They allow themselves to wander about from one communion to another, or from church to meeting-house, and make it a boast that they belong to no party and are above all parties; and argue, that provided men agree in some principal doctrines of the Gospel, it matters little whether they agree in any thing besides.

But those who boast of belonging to no party, and think themselves enlightened in this same confident boasting, I would, in all charity, remind that our Saviour Himself constituted what they must, on their principles, admit to be a party; that the Christian Church is simply and literally a party or society instituted by Christ. He bade us keep together. Fellowship with each other, mutual sympathy, and what spectators from without call party-spirit, all this is a prescribed duty; and the sin and the mischief arise,

[VII]   R

not from having a party, but in having many parties,
in separating from that one body or party which He has
appointed; for when men split the one Church of Christ
into fragments, they are doing their part to destroy it
altogether.

But while the Church of Christ is literally what the
world calls a party, it is something far higher also.   It
is not an institution of man, not a mere political establishment, not a creature of the state, depending on the
state's breath, made and unmade at its will, but it is
a Divine society, a great work of God, a true relic of
Christ and His Apostles, as Elijah's mantle upon Elisha,
a bequest which He has left us, and which we must
keep for His sake; a holy treasure which, like the ark
of Israel, looks like a thing of earth, and is exposed to
the ill-usage and contempt of the world, but which in
its own time, and according to the decree of Him who
gave it, displays to-day, and to-morrow, and the third
day, its miracles, as of mercy so of judgment, "light-
nings, and voices, and thunderings, and an earthquake,
and great hail."

SERMON XVIII.

STEDFASTNESS IN THE OLD PATHS.

JER. vi. 16.

" Thus saith the Lord, Stand ye in the ways, and see, and ask for the old paths, where is the good way, and walk therein, and ye shall find rest for your souls."

REVERENCE for the old paths is a chief Christian duty. We look to the future indeed with hope; yet this need not stand in the way of our dwelling on the past days of the Church with affection and deference. This is the feeling of our own Church, as continually expressed in the Prayer Book;—not to slight what has gone before, not to seek after some new thing, not to attempt discoveries in religion, but to keep what has once for all been committed to her keeping, and to be at rest.

Now it may be asked, " Why should we for ever be looking back at past times? were men perfect then? is it not possible to improve on the knowledge then possessed?" Let us examine this question.

In what respect should we follow old times? Now

here there is this obvious maxim—what God has given us from heaven cannot be improved, what man discovers for himself does admit of improvement: we follow old times then *so far* as God has spoken in them; but in those respects in which God has not spoken in them, we are not bound to follow them. Now what is the knowledge which God has *not* thought fit to reveal to us? *knowledge connected merely with this present world.* All this we have been left to acquire for ourselves. Whatever may have been told to Adam in paradise, or to Noah, about which we know nothing, still at least since that time no divinely authenticated directions (it would appear) have been given to the world at large, on subjects relating merely to this our temporal state of being. How we may till our lands and increase our crops; how we may build our houses, and buy and sell and get gain; how we may cross the sea in ships; how we may make "fine linen for the merchant," or, like Tubal-Cain, be artificers in brass and iron: as to these objects of this world, necessary indeed for the time, not everlastingly important, God has given us no clear instruction. He has not set His sanction here upon any rules of art, and told us what is best. They have been found out by man (as far as we know), and improved by man; and the first essays, as might be expected, were the rudest and least successful. Here then we have no need to follow the old ways. Besides, in many of these arts and pursuits, there is really neither right nor wrong at all; but the good varies with times and places. Each country has its own way, which is best for itself, and bad for others.

Again, God has given us no authority in questions of science. The heavens above, and the earth under our feet, are full of wonders, and have within them their own vast history. But the knowledge of the secrets they contain, the tale of their past revolutions, is not given us from Divine revelation; but left to man to attain by himself. And here again, since discovery is difficult, the old knowledge is generally less sure and complete than the modern knowledge. If we wish to boast about little matters, *we* know more about the motions of the heavenly bodies than Abraham, whose seed was in number as the stars; we can measure the earth, and fathom the sea, and weigh the air, more accurately than Moses, the inspired historian of the creation; and we can discuss the varied inhabitants of this globe better than Solomon, though " he spake of trees, from the cedar that is in Lebanon, even unto the hyssop that springeth out of the wall . . . . and of beasts, and of fowl, and of creeping things, and of fishes [1]." The world is more learned in these things than of old, probably will learn more still; a vast prospect is open to it, and an intoxicating one. Like the children of Cain, before the flood came and destroyed them all, men may increase and abound in such curious or merely useful

[1] 1 Kings iv. 33.

knowledge; nay, there is no limit to the progress of the human mind here; we may build us a city and a tower, whose top may reach almost to the very heavens.

Such is the knowledge which time has perfected, and in which the old paths are commonly the least direct and safe. But let us turn to that knowledge which God has given, and which therefore does not admit of improvement by lapse of time; this is *religious knowledge*. Here, whether a man might or might not have found out the truth for himself, or how far he was able without Divine assistance, waiving this question, which is nothing to the purpose, as a fact it has been from the beginning given him by revelation. God taught Adam how to please Him, and Noah, and Abraham, and Job. He has taught every nation all over the earth sufficiently for the moral training of every individual. In all these cases, the world's part of the work has been to pervert the truth, not to disengage it from obscurity. The new ways are the crooked ones. The nearer we mount up to the time of Adam, or Noah, or Abraham, or Job, the purer light of truth we gain; as we recede from it we meet with superstitions, fanatical excesses, idolatries, and immoralities. So again in the case of the Jewish Church, since God expressly gave the Jews a precise law, it is clear man could not improve upon it; he could but add the "traditions of men." Nothing was to be looked for from the cultivation of the human mind. "To the law and to the testimony" was the appeal;

and any deviation from it was, not a sign of increasing illumination, but " because there was no light " in the authors of innovation. Lastly, in the Christian Church, we cannot add or take away, as regards the doctrines that are contained in the inspired volume, as regards the faith once delivered to the saints. " Other foundation can no man lay than that is laid, which is Jesus Christ [1]."

But it may be said that, though the word of God is an infallible rule of faith, yet it requires interpreting, and why, as time goes on, should we not discover in it more than we at present know on the subject of religion and morals?

But this is hardly a question of practical importance to us as individuals; for in truth a very little knowledge is enough for teaching a man his duty : and, since Scripture is intended to teach us our duty, surely it was never intended as a storehouse of mere knowledge. Discoveries then in the details of morals and religion, by means of the inspired volume, whether possible or not, must not be looked out for, as the expectation may unsettle the mind; and take it off from matters of duty. Certainly all curious questions at least are forbidden us by Scripture, even though Scripture may be found adequate to answer them.

This should be insisted on. Do we think to become better men by knowing more? Little knowledge is

[1] 1 Cor. iii. 11.

required for religious obedience. The poor and rich, the learned and unlearned, are here on a level. We have all of us the means of doing our duty; we have not the *will,* and this no knowledge can give. We have need to subdue our own minds, and this no other person *can* do for us. The case is different in matters of learning and science. There others can and do labour for us; *we* can make use of *their* labours; we begin where they ended; thus things progress, and each successive age knows more than the preceding. But in religion each must begin, go on, and end, for himself. The religious history of each individual is as solitary and complete as the history of the world. Each man will, of course, gain more knowledge as he studies Scripture more, and prays and meditates more; but he cannot make another man wise or holy by his own advance in wisdom or holiness. When children cease to be born children, because they are born late in the world's history, when we can reckon the world's past centuries for the age of this generation, then only can the world increase in real excellence and truth as it grows older. The character will always require forming, evil will ever need rooting out of each heart; the grace to go before and to aid us in our moral discipline must ever come fresh and immediate from the Holy Spirit. So the world ever remains in its infancy, as regards the cultivation of moral truth; for the knowledge required for practice is little, and admits of little increase, except in the case of individuals, and then to them alone; and it cannot be handed on to another. "As it was in the beginning, is now, and ever shall be," such is the general history of man's moral discipline, running parallel to the unchanging glory of that All-Perfect God, who is its Author and Finisher.

Practical religious knowledge, then, is a personal gift, and, further, a gift from God; and, therefore, as experience has hitherto shown, more likely to be obscured than advanced by the lapse of time. But further, we know of the existence of an evil principle in the world, corrupting and resisting the truth in its measure, according to the truth's clearness and purity. Whether it be from the sinfulness of our nature, or from the malignity of Satan, striving with peculiar enmity against Divine truth, certain it is that the best gifts of God have been the most woefully corrupted. It was prophesied from the beginning, that the serpent should bruise the heel of Him who was ultimately to triumph over him; and so it has ever been. Our Saviour, who was the Truth itself, was the most spitefully entreated of all by the world. It has been the case with His followers too. He was crucified with thieves; *they* have been united and blended against their will with the worst and basest of mankind. The purer and more precious the gift which God bestows on us, far from this being a security for its abiding and increasing, rather the more grievously has that gift been abused.

St. John even seems to make the greater wickedness in the world the clear consequence and evidence of our Lord's having made His appearing. "Little children, it is the last time" (i. e. the time of the Christian Dispensation) : "and as ye have heard that Antichrist shall come, even now are there many Antichrists, *whereby we know* that it is the last time [1]." St. Paul drew the same picture. So far from anticipating brighter times in store for the Church before the end, he portends evil only. "This know" (he says to Timothy), "that in the last days perilous times will come. . . . . Evil men and seducers shall wax worse and worse, deceiving and being deceived [2]." In these and other passages surely there is no encouragement to look out for a more enlightened, peaceful, and pure state of the Church than it enjoys at present : rather, there is a call on us to consider the old and original way as the best, and all deviations from it, though they seem to promise an easier, safer, and shorter road, yet as really either tending another way, or leading to the right object with much hazard and many obstacles.

Such is the case as regards the knowledge of our duty,—that kind of knowledge which alone is really worth earnest seeking. And there is an important reason why we should acquiesce in it ;—because the conviction that things are so has no slight influence in forming our minds into that perfection of the religious

---

[1] 1 John ii. 18.   [2] 2 Tim. iii. 13.

character, at which it is our duty ever to be aiming. While we think it possible to make some great and important improvements in the subject of religion, we shall be unsettled, restless, impatient; we shall be drawn from the consideration of improving ourselves, and from using the day while it is given us, by the visions of a deceitful hope, which promises to make rich but tendeth to penury. On the other hand, if we feel that the way is altogether closed against discoveries in religion, as being neither practicable nor desirable, it is likely we shall be drawn more entirely and seriously to our own personal advancement in holiness; our eyes, being withdrawn from external prospects, will look more at home. We shall think less of circumstances, and more of our duties under them, whatever they are. In proportion as we cease to be theorists we shall become practical men ; we shall have less of self-confidence and arrogance, more of inward humility and diffidence ; we shall be less likely to despise others, and shall think of our own intellectual powers with less complacency.

It is one great peculiarity of the Christian character to be dependent. Men of the world, indeed, in proportion as they are active and enterprising, boast of their independence, and are proud of having obligations to no one. But it is the Christian's excellence to be diligent and watchful, to work and persevere, and yet to be in spirit *dependent ;* to be willing to serve, and to rejoice in the permission to do so ; to be content to view himself in a

subordinate place; to love to sit in the dust.   Though in
the Church a son of God, he takes pleasure in considering himself Christ's " servant " and " slave;" he feels
glad whenever he can put himself to shame.   So it is
the natural bent of his mind freely and affectionately to
visit and trace the footsteps of the saints, to sound the
praises of the great men of old who have wrought wonders in the Church and whose words still live; being
jealous of their honour, and feeling it to be even too
great a privilege for such as he is to be put in trust
with the faith once delivered to them, and following
them strictly in the narrow way, even as they have
followed Christ.   To the ears of such persons the words
of the text are as sweet music : " Thus saith the Lord,
Stand ye in the ways, and see, and ask for the old
paths, where is the good way, and walk therein, and ye
shall find rest for your souls."

The history of the Old Dispensation affords us a remarkable confirmation of what I have been arguing from
these words; for in the time of the Law there was an
increase of religious knowledge by fresh revelations.
From the time of Samuel especially to the time of
Malachi, the Church was bid look forward for a grow-
ing illumination, which, though not necessary for religious obedience, subserved the establishment of religious
comfort.   Now, I wish you to observe how careful the
inspired prophets of Israel are to prevent any kind of
disrespect being shown to the memory of former times,

on account of that increase of religious knowledge with which the later ages were favoured; and if such reverence for the past were a duty among the Jews when the Saviour was still to come, much more is it the duty of Christians, who expect no new revelation, and who, though they look forward in hope, yet see the future only in the mirror of times and persons past, who (in the Angel's words) " wait for that same Jesus : . . . . so to come in like manner as they saw Him go into heaven."

Now, as to the reverence enjoined and taught the Jews towards persons and times past, we may notice first the commandment given them to honour and obey their parents and elders. This, indeed, is a natural law. But that very circumstance surely gives force to the express and repeated injunctions given them to observe it, sanctioned too (as it was) with a special promise. Natural affection might have taught it; but it was rested by the Law on a higher sanction. Next, this duty of reverently regarding past times was taught by such general injunctions (more or less express) as the text. It is remarkable, too, when Micah would tell the Jews that the legal sacrifices appointed in time past were inferior to the moral duties, he states it not as a new truth, but refers to its announcement by a prophet in Moses' age,—to the answer of Balaam to Balak, king of Moab.

But, further, to bind them to the observance of this

duty, the past was made the pledge of the future, hope
was grounded upon memory; all prayer for favour sent
them back to the old mercies of God. "The Lord *hath
been* mindful of us, He *will* bless us[1];" this was the
form of their humble expectation. The favour vouchsafed to Abraham and Israel, and the deliverance from
Egypt, were the objects on which hope dwelt, and were
made the types of blessings in prospect. For instance,
out of the many passages which might be cited, Isaiah
says, "Awake . . . O arm of the Lord, *as in the ancient
days, in the generations of old[2].*" Micah, "Feed thy
people with thy rod, the flock of thine heritage, which
dwell solitary in the wood, in the midst of Carmel ; let
them feed in Bashan and Gilead, *as in the days of old ;
according to the days of thy coming out of Egypt will
I show unto him marvellous things[3].*" The Psalms
abound with like references to past mercies, as pledges
and types of future. Prophesying of the reign of
Christ, David says, "The Lord said, I will bring again
from Bashan, I will bring My people again from the
depths of the sea," and Moses too, speaking to the
Israelites—"*Remember the days of old,* consider the years
of many generations ; ask thy father and he will show
thee ; thy elders, and they will tell thee[4]." Accordingly, while a coming Saviour was predicted, still the
claims of past times on Jewish piety were maintained,

[1] Ps. cxv. 12.
[3] Micah vii. 14, 15.
[2] Isa. li. 9.
[4] Deut. xxxii. 7.

by His being represented by the prophets under the name and character of David, or in the dress and office of Aaron; so that, the clearer the revelation of the glory in prospect, in the same degree greater honour was put upon the former Jewish saints who typified it. In like manner the blessings promised to the Christian Church are granted to it in the character of Israel, or of Jerusalem, or of Sion.

Lastly, as Moses directed the eyes of his people towards the line of prophets which the Lord their God was to raise up from among them, ending in the Messiah, they in turn dutifully exalt Moses, whose system they were superseding. Samuel, David, Isaiah, Micah, Jeremiah, Daniel, Ezra, Nehemiah, each in succession, bear testimony to Moses. Malachi, the last of the prophets, while predicting the coming of John the Baptist, still gives this charge, " *Remember ye the law of Moses*, My servant, which I commanded unto him in Horeb for all Israel, with the statutes and judgments [1]." In like manner in the New Testament the last of the prophets and apostles describes the saints as singing " the song of Moses, the servant of God" (this is his honourable title, as elsewhere), " *and* the song of the Lamb [2]." Above all, our blessed Lord Himself sums up the whole subject we have been reviewing, both the doctrine and Jewish illustration of it, in His own authoritative words,—" If they hear not Moses and the

[1] Mal. iv. 4.   [2] Rev. xv. 3.

prophets, neither will they be persuaded, though one rose from the dead [1]." After this sanction, it is needless to refer to the reverence with which St. Paul regards the law of Moses, and to the commemoration he has made of the Old Testament saints in the eleventh chapter of his Epistle to the Hebrews.

Oh that we had duly drunk into this spirit of reverence and godly fear! Doubtless we are far above the Jews in our privileges; we are favoured with the news of redemption; we know doctrines, which righteous men of old time earnestly desired to be told, and were not. To us is revealed the Eternal Son, the Only-begotten of the Father, full of grace and truth. We are branches of the True Vine, which is sprung out of the earth and spread abroad. We have been granted Apostles, Prophets, Evangelists, pastors, and teachers. We celebrate those true Festivals which the Jews possessed only in shadow. For us Christ has died; on us the Spirit has descended. In these respects we are honoured and privileged, oh how far above all ages before He came! Yet our honours are our shame, when we contrast the glory given us with our love of the world, our fear of men, our lightness of mind, our sensuality, our gloomy tempers. What need have we to look with wonder and reverence at those saints of the Old Covenant, who with less advantages yet so far surpassed us; and still more at those of the Christian Church, who

[1] Luke xvi. 31.

both had higher gifts of grace and profited by them ! What need have we to humble ourselves; to pray God not to leave us, though we have left Him ; to pray Him to give us back what we have lost, to receive a repentant people, to renew in us a right heart and give us a religious will, and to enable us to follow Him perseveringly in His narrow and humbling way.

END OF VOL. VII.

LONDON :
GILBERT AND RIVINGTON, PRINTERS,
ST. JOHN'S SQUARE.

October, 1868.

New Works

IN COURSE OF PUBLICATION

BY

Messrs. RIVINGTON,

WATERLOO PLACE, LONDON;

HIGH STREET, OXFORD; TRINITY STREET, CAMBRIDGE.

Newman's (J.H.) Parochial and Plain
Sermons.
    Edited by the Rev. **W. J. Copeland,** Rector of Farnham,
Essex. From the Text of the last Editions published by
Messrs. Rivington.
    8 vols. Crown 8vo. 5*s.* each. (*Vols. I. to VI. just pub-
lished.*)

The Witness of the Old Testament to
Christ. The Boyle Lectures for the Year 1868.
    By the Rev. **Stanley Leathes,** M.A., Preacher at St. James's,
Westminster, and Professor of Hebrew in King's College,
London. 8vo. 9*s.*

London, Oxford, and Cambridge

A

The Reformation of the Church of
England ; its History, Principles, and Results. A.D. 1514—1547.
By **John Henry Blunt**, M.A.
8vo.   (*Nearly ready.*)

The Divinity of our Lord and Saviour
Jesus Christ ; being the Bampton Lectures for 1866.
By **Henry Parry Liddon**, M.A., Student of Christ Church,
Prebendary of Salisbury, and Examining Chaplain to the Bishop
of Salisbury.
Third Edition.   Crown 8vo.   5*s*.

Preparation for Death.
Translated from the Italian : forming the Advent Volume of
the " Ascetic Library."
Square Crown 8vo.   (*Nearly ready.*)

Five Years' Church Work in the King-
dom of Hawaii.
By the **Bishop of Honolulu.**
With Map and Illustrations.   Crown 8vo.   5*s*.

From Morning to Evening :
a Book for Invalids.
From the French of M. L'Abbé Henri Perreyve.   Translated
and adapted by an Associate of the Sisterhood of S. John
Baptist, Clewer.
Small 8vo.   5*s*.

London, Oxford, and Cambridge

The Virgin's Lamp:

Prayers and Devout Exercises for English Sisters, chiefly composed and selected by the late Rev. **J. M. Neale**, D.D., Founder of St. Margaret's, East Grinstead.

Small 8vo. 3s. 6d.

Perranzabuloe, the Lost Church Found;

or, The Church of England not a new Church, but Ancient, Apostolical, and Independent, and a Protesting Church Nine Hundred Years before the Reformation.

By the Rev. **C. Collins Trelawny**, M.A., formerly Rector of Timsbury, Somerset, and late Fellow of Balliol College, Oxford. With Illustrations.

New Edition. Crown 8vo. 3s. 6d.

Spiritual Life.

By **John James**, D.D., Canon of Peterborough, Author of a "Comment on the Collects of the Church of England."

12mo. (*Nearly ready.*)

Bible Readings for Family Prayer.

By the Rev. **W. H. Ridley**, M.A., Rector of Hambleden.
Old Testament—Genesis and Exodus.
New Testament—St. Luke and St. John.
In 2 Parts. Crown 8vo. (*Nearly ready.*)

The Doctrine of the Church of England,

as stated in Ecclesiastical Documents set forth by Authority of Church and State, in the Reformation Period between 1536 and 1662.

8vo. (*Nearly ready.*)

Selections from Modern French Authors.

With English Notes.

By **Henri Van Laun**, French Master at Cheltenham College.

Part 1.—Honoré de Balzac.

Crown 8vo.   3*s.* 6*d.*   (*Nearly ready.*)

Miscellaneous Poems.

By **Henry Francis Lyte**, M.A., Late Vicar of Lower Brixham, Devon.

New Edition.   Small 8vo.   5*s.*

A Key to the Knowledge and Use of the Holy Bible.

By **John Henry Blunt**, M.A.

Small 8vo.   2*s.* 6*d.*

Vox Ecclesiæ Anglicanæ: on the Church Ministry and Sacraments.

A Selection of Passages from the Writings of the Chief Divines of the Church of England. With short Introductions and Notices of the Writers.

By **George G. Perry**, M.A., Prebendary of Lincoln, Rector of Waddington, Rural Dean, and Proctor for the Diocese of Lincoln.

Crown 8vo.   6*s.*

England v. Rome: a Brief Handbook of the Roman Catholic Controversy, for the use of Members of the English Church.

By **H. B. Swete**, M.A., Fellow of Gonville and Caius College, Cambridge.

16mo.   (*Nearly ready.*)

Manual of Family Devotions, arranged

from the Book of Common Prayer.

By the Hon. **Augustus Duncombe**, D.D., Dean of York.
Printed in red and black.   Small 8vo.   3s. 6d.

Sketches of the Rites and Customs of

the Greco-Russian Church.

By **H. C. Romanoff.** With an Introductory Notice by the
Author of "The Heir of Redclyffe."

Crown 8vo.   7s. 6d.

Annals of the Bodleian Library, Ox-

ford, from its Foundation to A.D. 1867 ; containing an Account
of the various collections of printed books and MSS. there preserved ; with a brief Preliminary Sketch of the earlier Library
of the University.

By **W. D. Macray**, M.A., Assistant in the Library, Chaplain
of Magdalen and New Colleges.

8vo.   12s.

A Key to the Knowledge and Use of

the Book of Common Prayer.

By **John Henry Blunt**, M.A.

Small 8vo.   2s. 6d.

The Mysteries of Mount Calvary.

By **Antonio de Guevara**.

Being the First Volume of the "Ascetic Library," a Series of
Translations of Spiritual Works for Devotional Reading from
Catholic Sources.   Edited by the Rev. **Orby Shipley**, M.A.

Square crown 8vo.   3s. 6d.

Vestiarivm Christianvm : the Origin

and Gradual Development of the Dress of the Holy Ministry in the Church, as evidenced by Monuments both of Literature and of Art, from the Apostolic Age to the present time.

By the Rev. **Wharton B. Marriott**, M.A., F.S.A. (sometime Fellow of Exeter College, Oxford, and Assistant-Master at Eton), Select Preacher in the University, and Preacher, by licence from the Bishop, in the Diocese of Oxford.

Royal 8vo.   38s.

The Annotated Book of Common

Prayer; being an Historical, Ritual, and Theological Commentary on the Devotional System of the Church of England.

Edited by **John Henry Blunt**, M.A.

Third Edition.   Imperial 8vo, 36s.   Large paper Edition, royal 4to, with large margin for Notes, 3l. 3s.

The Prayer Book Interleaved ;

with Historical Illustrations and Explanatory Notes arranged parallel to the Text, by the Rev. **W. M. Campion**, B.D., Fellow and Tutor of Queens' College and Rector of St. Botolph's, and the Rev. **W. J. Beamont**, M.A., Fellow of Trinity College, Cambridge, and Incumbent of St. Michael's, Cambridge. With a Preface by the **Lord Bishop of Ely.**

Fourth Edition.   Small 8vo.   7s. 6d.

Flowers and Festivals ; or, Directions

for the Floral Decorations of Churches. With coloured Illustrations.

By **W. A. Barrett**, of S. Paul's Cathedral, late Clerk of Magdalen College, and Commoner of S. Mary Hall, Oxford.

Square crown 8vo.   5s.

Proceedings at the laying of the First

Stone of Keble College, Oxford, on St. Mark's Day, April 25th, 1868.

Small 4to. 3s. 6d.

Selections from Aristotle's Organon.

Edited by **John R. Magrath**, M.A., Fellow and Tutor of Queen's College, Oxford.

Crown 8vo. 3s. 6d.

Curious Myths of the Middle Ages.

By **S. Baring-Gould**, M.A., Author of "Post-Mediæval Preachers," &c. With Illustrations.

First Series. *Second Edition.* Crown 8vo. 7s. 6d.
Second Series. *Second Edition.* Crown 8vo. 9s. 6d.

Household Theology: a Handbook of

Religious Information respecting the Holy Bible, the Prayer Book, the Church, the Ministry, Divine Worship, the Creeds, &c. &c.

By **J. H. Blunt**, M.A.

Third Edition. Small 8vo. 3s. 6d.

Consoling Thoughts in Sickness.

Edited by **Henry Bailey**, B.D., Warden of St. Augustine's College, Canterbury.

Large type. Small 8vo. 2s. 6d.

Scripture Acrostics.

By the Author of "The Last Sleep of the Christian Child."
With Key.   Square 16mo.   2s.

The Sacraments and Sacramental Or-

dinances of the Church ; being a Plain Exposition of their
History, Meaning, and Effects.
By **John Henry Blunt**, M.A.
Small 8vo.   4s. 6d.

Queen Bertha and her Times.

By **E. H. Hudson**.
Small 8vo.   5s.

Catechesis ; or, Christian Instruction

preparatory to Confirmation and First Communion.
By **Charles Wordsworth**, D.C.L., Bishop of St. Andrew's.
New and cheaper Edition.   Small 8vo.   2s.

The Life and Times of S. Gregory the

Illuminator, Patron Saint and Founder of the Armenian
Church.
By **S. C. Malan**, M.A., Vicar of Broadwindsor.
8vo.   10s. 6d.

London, Oxford, and Cambridge

The Annual Register: a Review of

Public Events at Home and Abroad, for the Year 1867 ; being the Fifth Volume of an improved Series.

8vo.　18s.

*** *The Volumes for* 1863, 1864, 1865, *and* 1866 *may be had, price* 18s. *each.*

Thomas à Kempis, Of the Imitation of

Christ : a carefully revised translation, elegantly printed with red borders.

16mo.　2s. 6d.

Also a cheap Edition, without the red borders, 1s., *or in Wrapper,* 6d.

The Rule and Exercises of Holy Living.

By **Jeremy Taylor**, D.D., Bishop of Down, and Connor, and Dromore.

A New Edition, elegantly printed with red borders.　16mo.
3s. 6d.　(*Just ready.*)

A Short and Plain Instruction for the

better Understanding of the Lord's Supper ; to which is annexed, the Office of the Holy Communion, with proper Helps and Directions.

By **Thomas Wilson**, D.D., late Lord Bishop of Sodor and Man.

New and complete Edition, elegantly printed with rubrics and borders in red.　16mo.　(*Nearly ready.*)

Aids to Prayer: a Course of Lectures

delivered at Holy Trinity Church, Paddington, on the Sunday mornings in Lent, 1868.

By **Daniel Moore**, M.A., Honorary Chaplain to the Queen, &c.

Crown 8vo.　4s. 6d.

London, Oxford, and Cambridge

The Greek Testament.

With English Notes, intended for the Upper Forms of Schools, and for Pass-men at the Universities.   Abridged from the larger work of the **Dean of Canterbury.**
In one Volume, Crown 8vo.   10s. 6d.   (*Nearly ready.*)

Thoughts on Personal Religion ; being

a Treatise on the Christian Life in its Two Chief Elements, Devotion and Practice.
By **Edward Meyrick Goulburn**, D.D., Dean of Norwich.
New Edition.   Small 8vo.   6s. 6d.
An edition for presentation, Two Volumes, small 8vo.   10s. 6d.
Also, a Cheap Edition.   3s. 6d.

Six Short Sermons on Sin.   Lent Lectures

at S. Alban the Martyr, Holborn.
By the Rev. **Orby Shipley**, M.A.
Fourth Edition.   Small 8vo.   1s.

Daily Devotions ; or, Short Morning

and Evening Services for the use of a Churchman's Household.
By the Ven. **Charles C. Clerke**, Archdeacon of Oxford.
18mo.   1s.

A Fourth Series of Parochial Sermons,

preached in a Village Church.
By the Rev. **Charles A. Heurtley**, D.D., Rector of Fenny Compton, Warwickshire, Margaret Professor of Divinity, and Canon of Christ Church, Oxford.
Small 8vo.   5s. 6d.

London, Oxford, and Cambridge

Popular Objections to the Book of

Common Prayer considered, in Four Sermons on the Sunday Lessons in Lent, the Commination Service, and the Athanasian Creed, with a Preface on the existing Lectionary.

By **Edward Meyrick Goulburn**, D.D., Dean of Norwich.

Small 8vo. 2s. 6d.

Sickness; its Trials and Blessings.

Fine Edition. Small 8vo. 3s. 6d.

Also, a Cheap Edition, 1s. 6d., or in Paper Wrapper, 1s.

Devotional Commentary on the Gospel

according to S. Matthew.

Translated from **Pasquier Quesnel**.

Crown 8vo. (*In the Press.*)

Flosculi Cheltonienses: a Selection

from the Cheltenham College Prize Poems, 1846—1866.

Edited by **C. S. Jerram**, M.A., Trinity College, Oxford, and **Theodore W. James**, M.A., Pembroke College, Oxford.

Crown 8vo. 9s.

The Dogmatic Faith: an Inquiry

into the Relation subsisting between Revelation and Dogma. Being the Bampton Lectures for 1867.

By **Edward Garbett**, M.A., Incumbent of Christ Church, Surbiton.

Second Edition. Crown 8vo. 5s.

London Ordination, Advent, 1867;

being Seven Addresses to the Candidates for Holy Orders, in December, 1867.

By **Archibald Campbell, Lord Bishop of London**, and his **Chaplains.**

Together with the Examination Papers.

8vo.   4s.

Family Prayers: compiled from various

sources (chiefly from Bishop Hamilton's Manual), and arranged on the Liturgical Principle.

By **Edward Meyrick Goulburn**, D.D., Dean of Norwich.

New Edition.   Crown 8vo, large type, 3s. 6d.   16mo, 1s.

Cheap Edition.

Eastern Orthodoxy in the Eighteenth

Century ; being a Correspondence between the Greek Patriarchs and the Nonjurors.

Edited, with an Introduction, by the Rev. **George Williams**, B.D., Senior Fellow of King's College, Cambridge.

8vo.   (*Nearly ready.*)

Catechetical Notes and Class Questions,

Literal and Mystical ; chiefly on the Earlier Books of Holy Scripture.

By the late Rev. **J. M. Neale**, D.D., Warden of Sackville College, East Grinstead.

Crown 8vo.   (*In the Press.*)

The Treasury of Devotion : a Manual

of Prayers for daily use.

Edited by the Rev. **T. T. Carter**, Rector of Clewer.

16mo.   (*In preparation.*)

London, Oxford, and Cambridge

Liber Precum Publicarum Ecclesiæ

Anglicanæ.

À **Gulielmo Bright**, A.M., et **Petro Goldsmith Medd**, A.M., Presbyteris, Collegii Universitatis in Acad. Oxon. Sociis, Latine redditus.

In an elegant pocket volume, with all the Rubrics in red. *New Edition.* Small 8vo. (*Nearly ready.*)

The Voice of the Good Shepherd to His

Lost Sheep; being an Exposition of the former part of the Parable of the Prodigal Son.

By **Robert G. Swayne**, M.A., Rector of St. Edmund's, Salisbury.

Small 8vo. 2s. 6d.

Counsels upon Holiness of Life.

Translated from the Spanish of "The Sinner's Guide" by **Luis de Granada**; forming a volume of the "Ascetic Library."
Crown 8vo. (*In preparation.*)

A Glossary of Ecclesiastical Terms;

containing Explanations of Terms used in Architecture, Ecclesiology, Hymnology, Law, Ritualism, Theology, Heresies, and Miscellaneous Subjects.

By Various Writers. Edited by the Rev. **Orby Shipley**, M.A.
8vo. (*In preparation.*)

Reflections on the Revolution in France,

and on the Proceedings in certain Societies in London relative to that Event. In a Letter intended to have been sent to a Gentleman in Paris, 1790.

By the Right Hon. **Edmund Burke**, M.P.
New Edition. With a short Biographical Notice. Crown 8vo. 3s. 6d.

London, Oxford, and Cambridge

Apostolical Succession in the Church
of England.

By the Rev. **Arthur W. Haddan**, B.D., Rector of Barton-on-the-Heath, and late Fellow of Trinity College, Oxford.

8vo. (*In preparation.*)

The Holy Bible.

With Notes and Introductions.

By **Chr. Wordsworth**, D.D., Archdeacon of Westminster.

			£	s.	d.
Vol. I. 38s.	I.	Genesis and Exodus. *Second Edit.*	1	1	0
	II.	Leviticus, Numbers, Deuteronomy. *Second Edition*	0	18	0
Vol. II. 21s.	III.	Joshua, Judges, Ruth. *Second Edit.*	0	12	0
	IV.	The Books of Samuel. *Second Edit.*	0	10	0
Vol. III. 21s.	V.	The Books of Kings, Chronicles, Ezra, Nehemiah, Esther. *Second Edition*	1	1	0
Vol. IV. 34s.	VI.	The Book of Job. *Second Edition.*	0	9	0
	VII.	The Book of Psalms. *Second Edit.*	0	15	0
	VIII.	Proverbs, Ecclesiastes, Song of Solomon	0	12	0
Vol. V.	IX.	Isaiah	0	12	6

Sermons preached before the University
of Oxford, chiefly during the years 1863—1865.

By **Henry Parry Liddon**, M.A., Student of Christ Church, Prebendary of Salisbury, Examining Chaplain to the Lord Bishop of Salisbury, and lately Select Preacher.

Second Edition. 8vo. 8s.

Stones of the Temple: a familiar

Explanation of the Fabric and Furniture of the Church, with Illustrations, engraved by **O. Jewitt.**

By the Rev. **Walter Field**, M.A., Vicar of Godmersham.

Post 8vo.   (*In preparation.*)

A Summary of Theology and Ecclesiastical History:

a Series of Original Works on all the principal subjects of Theology and Ecclesiastical History.

By Various Writers.

In 8 Vols., 8vo.   (*In preparation.*)

Parish Musings; or, Devotional Poems.

By **John S. B. Monsell**, LL.D., Vicar of Egham, Surrey, and Rural Dean.

Tenth Edition.   18mo, 1s., or, in limp cloth, 1s. 6d.
A superior Edition may be had, in small 8vo, 2s. 6d.

Standing and Stumbling.

Part   I.—Seven Common Faults.
Part II.—Your Duty and Mine.
Part III.—Things Rarely Met With.

By **James Erasmus Philipps**, M.A., Vicar of Warminster.

Small 8vo.   2s. 6d.

(*The Parts may be had separately, 1s. each.*)

An Outline of Logic,

for the use of Teachers and Students.

By **Francis Garden**, M.A., Trinity College, Cambridge, Sub-Dean of Her Majesty's Chapels Royal; Chaplain to the Household in St. James' Palace; Professor of Mental and Moral Science, Queen's College, London.

Small 8vo.   4s.

An Introduction to the Devotional

Study of the Holy Scriptures.

By **Edward Meyrick Goulburn**, D.D., Dean of Norwich.

Ninth Edition. Small 8vo. 3*s.* 6*d.*

The London Diocese Book for 1868

(fourth year of issue), under the sanction of the Lord Bishop of London.

Crown 8vo. In wrapper, 1*s.*

On Miracles; being the Bampton

Lectures for 1865.

By **J. B. Mozley**, B.D., Vicar of Old Shoreham, late Fellow of Magdalen College, Oxford.

Second Edition. 8vo. 10*s.* 6*d.*

Sermons on Unity; with an Essay on

Religious Societies, and a Lecture on the Life and Times of Wesley.

By **F. C. Massingberd**, M.A., Chancellor of Lincoln.

Crown 8vo. 3*s.* 6*d.*

Songs of Joy for the Age of Joy.

By the Rev. **John P. Wright**, B.A.

18mo. 6*d.*

Semele; or, The Spirit of Beauty:

a Venetian Tale.

By **J. D. Mereweather**, B.A. Oxon., English Chaplain at Venice.

Small 8vo. 3*s.* 6*d.*

London, Oxford, and Cambridge

Warnings of the Holy Week, &c.;

being a Course of Parochial Lectures for the Week before Easter and the Easter Festivals.

By the Rev. **W. Adams**, M.A., late Vicar of St. Peter's-in-the-East, Oxford, and Fellow of Merton College.

Sixth Edition.   Small 8vo.   4s. 6d.

Farewell Counsels of a Pastor to his

Flock, on Topics of the Day: Nine Sermons preached at St. John's, Paddington.

By **Edward Meyrick Goulburn**, D.D., Dean of Norwich.

Third Edition.   Small 8vo.   4s.

An Illuminated Edition of the Book of

Common Prayer, printed in Red and Black, on fine toned Paper; with Borders and Titles, designed after the manner of the 14th Century, by **R. R. Holmes**, F.S.A., and engraved by **O. Jewitt**.

Crown 8vo.   White vellum cloth illuminated.   16s.

This Edition of the PRAYER BOOK *may be had in various Bindings for presentation.*

Yesterday, To-day, and For Ever: a

Poem in Twelve Books.

By **Edward Henry Bickersteth**, M.A., Incumbent of Christ Church, Hampstead, and Chaplain to the Bishop of Ripon.

Second and Cheaper Edition.   Small 8vo.   6s.

The Gate of Paradise: a Dream of

Easter Eve.   With Frontispiece.

Square crown 8vo.   6d.

The Greek Testament.

With Notes and Introductions.
By **Chr. Wordsworth**, D.D., Archdeacon of Westminster.
2 Vols.　Impl. 8vo.　4*l*.

The Parts may be had separately, as follows :—
The Gospels, 6*th Edition*, 21*s*.
The Acts, 5*th Edition*, 10*s*. 6*d*.
St. Paul's Epistles, 5*th Edition*, 31*s*. 6*d*.
General Epistles, Revelation, and Indexes, 3*rd Edition*, 21*s*.

The Acts of the Deacons; being a

Course of Lectures, Critical and Practical, upon the Notices of St. Stephen and St. Philip the Evangelist, contained in the Acts of the Apostles.
By **Edward Meyrick Goulburn**, D.D., Dean of Norwich.
Second Edition.　Small 8vo.　6*s*.

Sermons for Children; being Twenty-

eight short Readings, addressed to the Children of St. Margaret's Home, East Grinstead.
By the late Rev. **J. M. Neale**, D.D., Warden of Sackville College.
Small 8vo.　3*s*.

Our Lord Jesus Christ Teaching on

the Lake of Gennesaret : Six Discourses suitable for Family Reading.
By **Charles Baker**, M.A., Oxon, Vicar of Appleshaw, Hants.
Small 8vo.　1*s*. 6*d*.

London, Oxford, and Cambridge

The Greek Testament.

With a Critically revised Text ; a Digest of Various Readings ; Marginal References to Verbal and Idiomatic Usage ; Prolegomena ; and a Critical and Exegetical Commentary. For the use of Theological Students and Ministers. By **Henry Alford**, D.D., Dean of Canterbury.

4 Vols. 8vo. 102*s.*

The Volumes are sold separately as follows :—

Vol. I.—The Four Gospels. *Sixth Edition.* 28*s.*
Vol. II.—Acts to II. Corinthians. *Fifth Edition.* 24*s.*
Vol. III.—Galatians to Philemon. *Fourth Edition.* 18*s.*
Vol. IV.—Hebrews to Revelation. *Third Edition.* 32*s.*

The New Testament for English

Readers ; containing the Authorized Version, with a revised English Text ; Marginal References ; and a Critical and Explanatory Commentary. By **Henry Alford**, D.D., Dean of Canterbury.

Now complete in 2 Vols. or 4 Parts, price 54*s.* 6*d.*
Separately,

Vol. 1, Part I.—The three first Gospels, with a Map. *Second Edition.* 12*s.*
Vol. 1, Part II.—St. John and the Acts. 10*s.* 6*d.*
Vol. 2, Part I.—The Epistles of St. Paul, with a Map. 16*s.*
Vol. 2, Part II.—Hebrews to Revelation. 8vo. 16*s.*

The Beatitudes of Our Blessed Lord,

considered in Eight Practical Discourses.
By the Rev. **John Peat**, M.A., of St. Peter's College, Cambridge, Vicar of East Grinstead, Sussex.

Small 8vo. 3*s.* 6*d.*

Arithmetic for the Use of Schools ;

with a numerous collection of Examples.

By **R. D. Beasley**, M.A., Head Master of Grantham Grammar School, and formerly Fellow of St. John's College, Cambridge ; Author of "Elements of Plane Trigonometry."

12mo. 3s.

The Examples are also sold separately:—Part I., Elementary Rules, 8d.   Part II., Higher Rules, 1s. 6d.

The Formation of Tenses in the Greek

Verb ; showing the Rules by which every Tense is Formed from the pure stem of the Verb, and the necessary changes before each Termination.   By **C. S. Jerram**, M.A., late Scholar of Trinity College, Oxon.

Crown 8vo.   1s. 6d.

Professor Inman's Nautical Tables,

for the use of British Seamen. *New Edition*, by the Rev. **J. W. Inman**, late Fellow of St. John's College, Cambridge, and Head Master of Chudleigh Grammar School.   Revised, and enlarged by the introduction of Tables of ½ log. haversines, log. differences, &c. ; with a more compendious method of Working a Lunar, and a Catalogue of Latitudes and Longitudes of Places on the Seaboard.

Royal 8vo.   21s.

Arithmetic, Theoretical and Practical ;

adapted for the use of Colleges and Schools.

By **W. H. Girdlestone**, M.A., of Christ's College, Cambridge.

Crown 8vo.   6s. 6d.

A Greek Primer for the use of Schools.

By the Rev. **Charles H. Hole**, M.A., Scholar of Worcester College, Oxford ; late Assistant Master at King Edward's School, Bromsgrove.

Crown 8vo.   4s.

Sacred Allegories :

The Shadow of the Cross—The Distant Hills—The Old Man's Home—The King's Messengers.

By the Rev. **W. Adams**, M.A., late Fellow of Merton College, Oxford. With Illustrations.

New Edition. Small 8vo. *5s.*

The Four Allegories are also published separately in 18mo., 1s. each in limp cloth.

Priest and Parish.

By the Rev. **Harry Jones**, M.A., Incumbent of St. Luke's, Berwick Street, Soho ; Author of "Life in the World."

Square crown 8vo. *6s. 6d.*

Private Devotions for School-boys ;

together with some Rules of Conduct given by a Father to his Son, on his going to School.

By **William Henry,** third **Lord Lyttelton**; revised and corrected by his Son, fourth **Lord Lyttelton.**

Fifth Edition. 32mo. *6d.*

The Office of the Most Holy Name :

Devotional Help for Young Persons.

By the Editor of "The Churchman's Guide to Faith," &c.

18mo. *2s. 6d.*

Henry's First Latin Book.

By **Thomas Kerchever Arnold**, M.A., late Rector of Lyndon, and formerly Fellow of Trinity College, Cambridge.

Twentieth Edition. 12mo. *3s.*

London, Oxford, and Cambridge

Hymns and Poems · for the Sick and

Suffering; in connexion with the Service for the Visitation of the Sick.   Selected from various Authors.

Edited by **T. V. Fosbery**, M.A., Vicar of St. Giles's, Reading.

This Volume contains 233 separate pieces; of which about 90 are by writers who lived prior to the 18th Century; the rest are Modern, and some of these original.   Amongst the names of the writers (between 70 and 80 in number) occur those of Sir J. Beaumont, Sir T. Browne, Elizabeth of Bohemia, Phineas Fletcher, George Herbert, Dean Hickes, Bishop Ken, Francis Quarles, George Sandys, Jeremy Taylor, Henry Vaughan, Sir H. Wotton; and of modern writers, Mrs. Barrett Browning, Bishop Wilberforce, Samuel Taylor Coleridge, William Wordsworth, Archbishop Trench. Rev. J. Chandler, Rev. J. Keble, Rev. H. F. Lyte, Rev. J. S. Monsell, Rev. J. Moultrie.

New and cheaper Edition.   Small 8vo.   3*s*. 6*d*.

Döderlein's Handbook of Latin Syno-

nymes.

Translated from the German, by **H. H. Arnold**, B.A.
Third Edition.   12mo.   4*s*.

The Church Builder: a Quarterly

Journal of Church Extension in England and Wales.   Published in connexion with "The Incorporated Church Building Society." Volume for 1868.

With Illustrations.   Crown 8vo.   1*s*. 6*d*.

A Christian View of Christian His-

tory, from Apostolic to Mediæval Times.

By **John Henry Blunt**, M.A.

Crown 8vo.   7*s*.

London, Oxford, and Cambridge

A Practical Introduction to Latin

Prose Composition : Part I.

By **Thomas Kerchever Arnold**, M.A., late Rector of Lyndon, and formerly Fellow of Trinity College, Cambridge.

Fourteenth Edition. 8vo. 6*s*. 6*d*.

A Practical Introduction to English

Prose Composition. An English Grammar for Classical Schools; with Questions, and a Course of Exercises.

By **Thomas Kerchever Arnold**, M.A., late Rector of Lyndon, and formerly Fellow of Trinity College, Cambridge.

Eighth Edition. 12mo. 4*s*. 6*d*.

A Plain and Short History of England

for Children : in Letters from a Father to his Son. With a Set of Questions at the end of each Letter.

By **George Davys**, D.D., late Bishop of Peterborough.

New Edition. 1*s*. 6*d*.

A Manual of Confirmation, comprising

—1. A General Account of the Ordinance. 2. The Baptismal Vow, and the English Order of Confirmation, with Short Notes, Critical and Devotional. 3. Meditations and Prayers on Passages of Holy Scripture, in connexion with the Ordinance. With a Pastoral Letter instructing Catechumens how to prepare themselves for their first Communion.

By **Edward Meyrick Goulburn**, D.D., Dean of Norwich.

Seventh Edition. Small 8vo. 1*s*. 6*d*.

London, Oxford, and Cambridge

Latin via English ;

being the Second Part of Spelling turned Etymology.

By **Thomas Kerchever Arnold**, M.A., late Rector of Lyndon, and formerly Fellow of Trinity College, Cambridge.

Third Edition. 12mo. 4*s.* 6*d.*

A Collection of English Exercises,

translated from the writings of Cicero, for Schoolboys to re-translate into Latin.

By **William Ellis**, M.A. ; re-arranged and adapted to the Rules of the Public School Latin Primer, by **John T. White**, D.D., joint Author of White and Riddle's Latin-English Dictionary.

12mo. 3*s.* 6*d.*

A complete Greek and English Lexicon

for the Poems of Homer, and the Homeridæ ; illustrating the domestic, religious, political, and military condition of the Heroic Age, and explaining the most difficult passages

By **G. Ch. Crusius.** Translated from the German, with corrections and additions, by **Henry Smith,** Professor of Languages in Marietta College. Revised and edited by **Thomas Kerchever Arnold**, M.A., late Rector of Lyndon, and formerly Fellow of Trinity College, Cambridge.

Third Edition. 12mo. 9*s.*

A copious Phraseological English-

Greek Lexicon ; founded on a work prepared by **J. W. Frädersdorff,** Ph. Dr., late Professor of Modern Languages, Queen's College, Belfast.

Revised, Enlarged, and Improved by the late **Thomas Kerchever Arnold,** M.A., formerly Fellow of Trinity College, Cambridge, and **Henry Browne,** M.A., Vicar of Pevensey, and Prebendary of Chichester.

Fourth Edition. 8vo. 21*s.*

NEW PAMPHLETS

ON THE IRISH CHURCH QUESTION.

BY THE BISHOP OF OSSORY.

The Case of the Established Church in Ireland. By
JAMES THOMAS O'BRIEN, D.D., Bishop of Ossory, Ferns, and Leighlin.
Third Edition. With Appendix. 8vo. 2s. 6d.
The Appendix may also be had separately, 1s.

BY LORD MAYO.

Speech delivered in the House of Commons, 10th
March, 1868, upon Mr. Maguire's Motion as to the State of Ireland. By the
Earl of MAYO. 8vo. 1s.

BY LORD REDESDALE.

Speech in the House of Lords on Friday, 17th July,
1868, on moving for a copy of the Coronation Oath; with a Reply to an
Article in the "Saturday Review." 8vo. 6d.

BY JOHN JEBB, D.D.

The Rights of the Irish Branch of the United
Church of England and Ireland Considered on Fundamental Principles,
Human and Divine. By JOHN JEBB, D.D., Rector of Peterstow, Prebendary
and Prælector of Hereford Cathedral, and one of the Proctors for the Clergy
of Hereford in the Convocation of Canterbury. *Second Edition.* 8vo. 1s.

BY THE REV. LORD O'NEILL AND THE REV. DR. LEE.

The Church in Ireland. 1. *The Difficulties of her*
Present Position Considered. By the Rev. Lord O'NEILL, of Shane's
Castle, formerly Prebendary of S. Michael's, Dublin. II. The Duty of
Churchmen in England and Ireland at this Crisis towards Her. By the
Rev. ALFRED T. LEE, LL.D., Rector of Ahoghill, and Chaplain to his
Excellency the Lord Lieutenant. Two Sermons, lately preached in the
Parish Church of Ahoghill, Diocese of Connor. *Second Edition.* 8vo. 6d.

———— ◆ ————

The Irish Difficulty. 1. *The Church Question.*
2. The Land Question. 3. The Education Question. Being a Review of the
Debate in the House of Commons on Mr. Maguire's Motion (March 10,
1868). By an OBSERVER. *Fifth Edition.* 8vo. 6d.

The Church, the Land, and the Constitution ; or,
Mr. Gladstone in the newly-reformed Parliament. *Second Edition.* 8vo. 6d.

London, Oxford, and Cambridge

NEW PAMPHLETS.

BY THE BISHOP OF WORCESTER.

A Charge delivered to the Clergy and Churchwardens of the Diocese of Worcester. By HENRY, Lord Bishop of WORCESTER, at his Visitation in June, 1868. 8vo. 1s. 6d.

BY THE BISHOP OF PERTH.

Christ's Spiritual Presence with His Worshippers the True Glory of His House: a Sermon preached in the New Parish Church of Stroud, Gloucestershire, on Wednesday, August 5, 1868 (the Morrow of the Consecration). By the Right Rev. MATTHEW HALE, D.D., Bishop of Perth. 12mo. 3d.

BY ARCHDEACON WORDSWORTH.

On the Proposed Council at Rome: an Address, at the Ordination of Priests and Deacons in the Diocese of Oxford, Sept. 20, 1868. By CHR. WORDSWORTH, D.D., Canon of Westminster, and Archdeacon. 8vo. 1s.

Sacred Music: a Sermon preached at the Anni- versary of the Choral Association of the Diocese of Llandaff, in the Cathedral Church of Llandaff, Sept. 2, 1868. By CHR. WORDSWORTH, D.D., Archdeacon of Westminster. 8vo. 6d.

BY ARCHDEACON BICKERSTETH.

A Charge delivered at his Tenth Visitation of the Archdeaconry of Buckingham, in June, 1868. By EDWARD BICKERSTETH, D.D., Prolocutor of the Lower House of Convocation of the Province of Canterbury, Archdeacon of Buckingham, Honorary Canon of Christ Church, and Vicar of Aylesbury. 8vo. 1s.

BY ARCHDEACON DENISON.

The Churches of England and Ireland one Church by identity of Divine Trust: a Paper read at a Special Meeting of the Irish Church Society, Dublin, Wednesday, September 30, 1868. By GEORGE ANTHONY DENISON, M.A., Vicar of East Brent, Archdeacon of Taunton. 8vo. 6d.

BY ARCHDEACON ROSE.

The Position of the Church of England as a National Church Historically Considered: being the Primary Charge of HENRY JOHN ROSE, B.D., Archdeacon of Bedford. 8vo. 1s.

BY THE REV. F. PIGOU.

The Power of Unostentatious Piety: a Sermon preached in St. Philip's Chapel, Regent Street, Sunday, June 14, and before the Queen and Royal Family, in the Private Chapel, Windsor Castle, Sunday, June 21. By FRANCIS PIGOU, M.A., F.R.G.S., Incumbent of St. Philip's. 8vo. 6d.

BY THE REV. JOHN MARTIN.

Bribery: a Sermon. By JOHN MARTIN, M.A., of Sidney Sussex College, and Vicar of St. Andrew the Great, Cambridge. 8vo. 6d.

London, Oxford, and Cambridge

CATENA CLASSICORUM,
A SERIES OF CLASSICAL AUTHORS,
EDITED BY MEMBERS OF BOTH UNIVERSITIES UNDER THE DIRECTION OF

THE REV. ARTHUR HOLMES, M.A.
FELLOW AND LECTURER OF CLARE COLLEGE, CAMBRIDGE, LECTURER AND LATE FELLOW OF ST. JOHN'S COLLEGE,

AND

THE REV. CHARLES BIGG, M.A.
LATE SENIOR STUDENT AND TUTOR OF CHRIST CHURCH, OXFORD, SECOND CLASSICAL MASTER OF CHELTENHAM COLLEGE.

The following Parts have been already published:—

SOPHOCLIS TRAGOEDIAE,
Edited by R. C. JEBB, M.A. Fellow and Assistant Tutor of Trinity College, Cambridge.
[Part I. The Electra. 3s. 6d.   Part II. The Ajax. 3s. 6d.

JUVENALIS SATIRAE,
Edited by G. A. SIMCOX, M.A. Fellow and Classical Lecturer of Queen's College, Oxford.   [Thirteen Satires. 3s. 6d.

THUCYDIDIS HISTORIA,
Edited by CHARLES BIGG, M.A. late Senior Student and Tutor of Christ Church, Oxford. Second Classical Master of Cheltenham College.
[Vol. I. Books I. and II. with Introductions. 6s.

DEMOSTHENIS ORATIONES PUBLICAE,
Edited by G. H. HESLOP, M.A. late Fellow and Assistant Tutor of Queen's College, Oxford. Head Master of St. Bees.
[Parts I. & II. The Olynthiacs and the Philippics. 4s. 6d.

ARISTOPHANIS COMOEDIAE,
Edited by W. C. GREEN, M.A. late Fellow of King's College, Cambridge. Classical Lecturer at Queens' College.
[Part I. The Acharnians and the Knights. 4s.
[Part II. The Clouds. 3s. 6d.
[Part III. The Wasps. (*Just ready.*)

ISOCRATIS ORATIONES,
Edited by JOHN EDWIN SANDYS, B.A. Fellow and Lecturer of St. John's College, and Lecturer at Jesus College, Cambridge.
[Part I. Ad Demonicum et Panegyricus. 4s. 6d.

CATENA CLASSICORUM—Opinions of the Press.

Mr. Jebb's Sophocles.

"Of Mr. Jebb's scholarly edition of the 'Electra' of Sophocles we cannot speak too highly. The whole Play bears evidence of the taste, learning, and fine scholarship of its able editor. Illustrations drawn from the literature of the Continent as well as of England, and the researches of the highest classical authorities are embodied in the notes, which are brief, clear, and always to the point."—*London Review, March 16, 1867.*

"The editorship of the work before us is of a very high order, displaying at once ripe scholarship, sound judgment, and conscientious care. An excellent Introduction gives an account of the various forms assumed in Greek literature by the legend upon which 'The Electra' is founded, and institutes a comparison between it and the 'Choephorae' of Æschylus. The text is mainly that of Dindorf. In the notes, which are admirable in every respect, is to be found exactly what is wanted, and yet they rather suggest and direct further inquiry than supersede exertion on the part of the student."—*Athenæum.*

"The Introduction proves that Mr. Jebb is something more than a mere scholar,—a man of real taste and feeling. His criticism upon Schlegel's remarks on the Electra are, we believe, new, and certainly just. As we have often had occasion to say in this Review, it is impossible to pass any reliable criticism upon school-books until they have been tested by experience. The notes, however, in this case appear to be clear and sensible, and direct attention to the points where attention is most needed."—*Westminster Review.*

"We have no hesitation in saying that in style and manner Mr. Jebb's notes are admirably suited for their purpose. The explanations of grammatical points are singularly lucid, the parallel passages generally well chosen, the translations bright and graceful, the analysis of arguments terse and luminous. Mr. Jebb has clearly shown that he possesses some of the qualities most essential for a commentator."—*Spectator*

"The notes appear to us exactly suited to assist boys of the Upper Forms at Schools, and University students; they give sufficient help without over-doing explanations. . . . . His critical remarks show acute and exact scholarship, and a very useful addition to ordinary notes is the scheme of metres in the choruses."—*Guardian.*

"If, as we are fain to believe, the editors of the *Catena Classicorum* have got together such a pick of scholars as have no need to play their best card first, there is a bright promise of success to their series in the first sample of it which has come to hand —Mr. Jebb's 'Electra.' We have seen it suggested that it is unsafe to pronounce on the merits of a Greek Play edited for educational purposes until it has been tested in the hands of pupils and tutors. But our examination of the instalment of, we hope, a complete 'Sophocles,' which Mr. Jebb has put forth, has assured us that this is a needless suspension of judgment, and prompted us to commit the justifiable rashness of pronouncing upon its contents, and of asserting after due perusal that it is calculated to be admirably serviceable to every class of scholars and learners. And this assertion is based upon the fact that it is a by no means one-sided edition, and that it looks as with the hundred eyes of Argus, here, there, and every where, to keep the reader from straying. In a

CATENA CLASSICORUM—Opinions of the Press.

concise and succinct style of English annotation, forming the best substitute for the time-honoured Latin notes which had so much to do with making good scholars in days of yore, Mr. Jebb keeps a steady eye for all questions of grammar, construction, scholarship, and philology, and handles these as they arise with a helpful and sufficient precision. In matters of grammar and syntax his practice for the most part is to refer his reader to the proper section of Madvig's 'Manual of Greek Syntax:' nor does he ever waste space and time in explaining a construction, unless it be such an one as is not satisfactorily dealt with in the grammars of Madvig or Jelf. Experience as a pupil and a teacher has probably taught him the value of the wholesome task of hunting out a grammar reference for oneself, instead of finding it, handy for slurring over, amidst the hundred and one pieces of information in a voluminous foot-note. But whenever there occurs any peculiarity of construction, which is hard to reconcile to the accepted usage, it is Mr. Jebb's general practice to be ready at hand with manful assistance."—*Contemporary Review.*

"Mr. Jebb has produced a work which will be read with interest and profit by the most advanced scholar, as it contains, in a compact form, not only a careful summary of the labours of preceding editors, but also many acute and ingenious original remarks. We do not know whether the matter or the manner of this excellent commentary is deserving of the higher praise : the skill with which Mr. Jebb has avoided, on the one hand, the wearisome prolixity of the Germans, and on the other the jejune brevity of the Porsonian critics, or the versatility which has enabled him in turn to elucidate the plots, to explain the verbal difficulties, and to illustrate the idioms of his author. All this, by a studious economy of space and a remarkable precision of expression, he has done for the 'Ajax' in a volume of some 200 pages."—*Athenæum.*

Mr. Simcox's Juvenal.

"Of Mr. Simcox's 'Juvenal' we can only speak in terms of the highest commendation, as a simple, unpretending work, admirably adapted to the wants of the school-boy or of a college passman. It is clear, concise, and scrupulously honest in shirking no real difficulty. The pointed epigrammatic hits of the satirist are every where well brought out, and the notes really are what they profess to be, explanatory in the best sense of the term."—*London Review.*

"This is a link in the *Catena Classicorum* to which the attention of our readers has been more than once directed as a good Series of Classical works for School and College purposes. The Introduction is a very comprehensive and able account of Juvenal, his satires, and the manuscripts."—*Athenæum.*

"This is a very original and enjoyable Edition of one of our favourite classics."—*Spectator.*

"Every class of readers—those who use Mr. Simcox as their sole interpreter, and those who supplement larger editions by his concise matter—will alike find interest and careful research in his able Preface. This indeed we should call the great feature of his book. The three facts which sum up Juvenal's history so far as we know it are soon despatched : but the internal evidence both as to the dates of his writing and publishing his Satires, and as to his character as a writer, occupy some fifteen or twenty pages, which will repay methodical study." — *Churchman.*

CATENA CLASSICORUM—Opinions of the Press.

Mr. Bigg's Thucydides.

"Mr. Bigg in his 'Thucydides' prefixes an analysis to each book, and an admirable introduction to the whole work, containing full information as to all that is known or related of Thucydides, and the date at which he wrote, followed by a very masterly critique on some of his characteristics as a writer."—*Athenæum.*

"While disclaiming absolute originality in his book, Mr. Bigg has so thoroughly digested the works of so many eminent predecessors in the same field, and is evidently on terms of such intimacy with his author as perforce to inspire confidence. A well-pondered and well-written introduction has formed a part of each link in the 'Catena' hitherto published, and Mr. Bigg, in addition to a general introduction, has given us an essay on 'Some Characteristics of Thucydides,' which no one can read without being impressed with the learning and judgment brought to bear on the subject."—*Standard.*

"We need hardly say that these books are carefully edited; the reputation of the editor is an assurance on this point. If the rest of the history is edited with equal care, it must become the standard book for school and college purposes."—*John Bull.*

"Mr. Bigg first discusses the facts of the life of Thucydides, then passes to an examination into the date at which Thucydides wrote; and in the third section expatiates on some characteristics of Thucydides. These essays are remarkably well written, are judicious in their opinions, and are calculated to give the student much insight into the work of Thucydides, and its relation to his own times, and to the works of subsequent historians."—*Museum.*

Mr. Heslop's Demosthenes.

"The usual introduction has in this case been dispensed with. The reader is referred to the works of Grote and Thirlwall for information on such points of history as arise out of these famous orations, and on points of critical scholarship to 'Madvig's Grammar,' where that is available, while copious acknowledgments are made to those commentators on whose works Mr. Heslop has based his own. Mr. Heslop's editions are, however, no mere compilations. That the points required in an oratorical style differ materially from those in an historical style, will scarcely be questioned, and accordingly we find that Mr. Heslop has given special care to those characteristics of style as well as of language, which constitute Demosthenes the very first of classic orators."—*Standard.*

"We must call attention to New Editions of various classics, in the excellent 'Catena Classicorum' series. The reputation and high standing of the editors are the best guarantees for the accuracy and scholarship of the notes."—*Westminster Review.*

"The notes are thoroughly good, so far as they go. Mr. Heslop has carefully digested the best foreign commentaries, and his notes are for the most part judicious extracts from them."—*Museum.*

"The annotations are scarcely less to be commended for the exclusion of superfluous matter than for the excellence of what is supplied. Well-known works are not quoted, but simply referred to, and information which ought to have been previously acquired is omitted."—*Athenæum.*

CATENA CLASSICORUM—Opinions of the Press.
Mr. Green's Aristophanes.

"The Editors of this Series have undertaken the task of issuing texts of all the authors commonly read, and illustrating them with an English Commentary, compendious as well as clear. If the future volumes fulfil the promise of the Prospectus as well as those already published, the result will be a very valuable work. The excellence of the print, and the care and pains bestowed upon the general getting up, form a marked contrast to the schoolbooks of our own day. Who does not remember the miserable German editions of classical authors in paper covers, execrably printed on detestable paper, which were thought amply good enough for the school-boys of the last generation? A greater contrast to these can hardly be imagined than is presented by the *Catena Classicorum*. Nor is the improvement only external : the careful revision of the text, and the notes, not too lengthy and confused, but well and judiciously selected, which are to be found in every page, add considerably to the value of this Edition, which we may safely predict will soon be an established favourite, not only among Schoolmasters, but at the Universities. The volume before us contains the first part of an Edition of Aristophanes which comprises the Acharnians and the Knights, the one first in order, and the other the most famous of the plays of the great Athenian Satirist."—*Churchman*.

"The utmost care has been taken with this Edition of the most sarcastic and clever of the old Greek dramatists, facilitating the means of understanding both the text and intention of that biting sarcasm which will never lose either point or interest, and is as well adapted to the present age as it was to the times when first put forward."—*Bell's Weekly Messenger*.

"The advantages conferred on the learner by these compendious aids can only be properly estimated by those who had experience of the mode of study years ago. The translated passages and the notes, while sufficient to assist the willing learner, cannot be regarded in any sense as *a cram*."—*Clerical Journal*.

"Mr. Green has discharged his part of the work with uncommon skill and ability. The notes show a thorough study of the two Plays, an independent judgment in the interpretation of the poet, and a wealth of illustration, from which the Editor draws whenever it is necessary."—*Museum*.

"Mr. Green presumes the existence of a fair amount of scholarship in all who read Aristophanes, as a study of his works generally succeeds to some considerable knowledge of the tragic poets. The notes he has appended are therefore brief, perhaps a little too brief. We should say the tendency of most modern editors is rather the other way ; but Mr. Green no doubt knows the class for which he writes, and has been careful to supply their wants."—*Spectator*.

"Mr. Green's admirable Introduction to 'The Clouds' of the celebrated comic poet deserves a careful perusal, as it contains an accurate analysis and many original comments on this remarkable play. The text is prefaced by a table of readings of Dindorf and Meineke, which will be of great service to students who wish to indulge in verbal criticism. The notes are copious and lucid, and the volume will be found useful for school and college purposes, and admirably adapted for private reading."—*Examiner*.

"Mr. Green furnishes an excellent Introduction to 'The Clouds' of Aristophanes, explaining the circumstances under which it was produced, and ably discussing the probable object of the author in writing it, which he considers to have been to put down the Sophists, a class whom Aristophanes thought dangerous to the morals of the community, and therefore caricatured in the person of Socrates,—not unnaturally, though irreverently, choosing him as their representative."—*Athenæum*.

CATENA CLASSICORUM.

The following Parts are in course of preparation:—

PLATONIS PHAEDO,

Edited by ALFRED BARRY, D.D. late Fellow of Trinity College, Cambridge, Principal of King's College, London.

DEMOSTHENIS ORATIONES PUBLICAE,

Edited by G. H. HESLOP, M.A. late Fellow and Assistant Tutor of Queen's College, Oxford. Head Master of St. Bees.
[Part II. De Falsâ Legatione.

MARTIALIS EPIGRAMMATA,

Edited by GEORGE BUTLER, M.A. Principal of Liverpool College; late Fellow of Exeter College, Oxford.

DEMOSTHENIS ORATIONES PRIVATAE,

Edited by ARTHUR HOLMES, M.A. Fellow and Lecturer of Clare College, Cambridge.   [Part I. De Coronâ.

HOMERI ILIAS,

Edited by S. H. REYNOLDS, M.A. Fellow and Tutor of Brasenose College, Oxford.   [Vol. I. Books I. to XII.

HORATI OPERA,

Edited by J. M. MARSHALL, M.A. Fellow and late Lecturer of Brasenose College, Oxford. One of the Masters in Clifton College.

TERENTI COMOEDIAE,

Edited by T. L. PAPILLON, M.A. Fellow and Classical Lecturer of Merton College, Oxford.

HERODOTI HISTORIA,

Edited by H. G. WOODS, M.A. Fellow and Tutor of Trinity College, Oxford.

TACITI HISTORIAE,

Edited by W. H. SIMCOX, M.A. Fellow and Lecturer of Queen's College, Oxford.

PERSII SATIRAE,

Edited by A. PRETOR, M.A., of Trinity College, Cambridge, Classical Lecturer of Trinity Hall, Composition Lecturer of the Perse Grammar School, Cambridge.

Check Out More Titles From HardPress Classics Series In this collection we are offering thousands of classic and hard to find books. This series spans a vast array of subjects – so you are bound to find something of interest to enjoy reading and learning about.

Subjects:
Architecture
Art
Biography & Autobiography
Body, Mind &Spirit
Children & Young Adult
Dramas
Education
Fiction
History
Language Arts & Disciplines
Law
Literary Collections
Music
Poetry
Psychology
Science
…and many more.

Visit us at www.hardpress.net